To _____

From _____

*Things I Want
My Daughters to Know*

ALSO BY ALEXANDRA STODDARD

Things I Want My Daughters to Know

A SMALL BOOK
ABOUT THE BIG ISSUES
IN LIFE

Alexandra Stoddard

Collins

An Imprint of HarperCollins*Publishers*

HarperCollins books may be purchased for educational, business, or sales promotional use. For information, please write: Special Markets Department, HarperCollins Publishers Inc., 10 East 53rd Street, New York, NY 10022.

The Elisabeth Kübler-Ross quote on page 70 is reprinted with the permission of Scribner, an imprint of Simon & Schuster Adult Publishing Group, from *On Death and Dying* by Elisabeth Kübler-Ross. Copyright © 1997 by Elisabeth Kübler-Ross.

First Collins hardcover edition published 2004
First Collins paperback edition published 2007

Designed by Leah Carlson-Stanisic

Printed on acid-free paper

ISBN: 978-00-6128436-6

The Library of Congress has catalogued the hardcover edition as follows:

Stoddard, Alexandra.
    Things I want my daughters to know: a small book about the big issues in life/ Alexandra Stoddard.
        p. cm.
ISBN: 978-06-059487-9
1. Women—Conduct of life. I. Title.

BJ160.S76 2004
170'.82—DC22   2004040546

07 08 09 10 ❖/RRD 10 9 8 7 6 5 4 3 2 1

This book is dedicated to

Alexandra and Brooke

with all my love.

❋

Acknowledgments

The idea for this book was conceived over lunch with my friend and literary agent, Carl Brandt. I felt a need to pass on some timeless wisdom to my daughters (and anyone else who will listen) to help them navigate their life's journey with a light on their path. After extensive discussion, Carl said, "Write the book." I now consider this book of essays a personal gift. I am grateful to you, Carl, for your vision and belief in me.

My editor, Toni Sciarra, loved the idea and helped me narrow down my 126 essays to 55. I have enormous trust and confidence in you. You brilliantly guided me to give the reader more without diluting the depth of the message. Congratulations on our tenth book that you have so wisely edited.

Sharon Scarpa, my loyal and thoughtful assistant, your skills are unmatched. You never complained as the written pages kept coming under tight deadlines. Because of your talent, you allow me my greatest joy—to be able to write my books longhand on smooth white paper using a favorite fountain pen. Thank you for the great contribution you make to my life's happiness.

I express sincere gratitude to all the wise people who continuously come into my consciousness, awakening my soul to see the tall oak tree in the acorn.

Contents

Foreword

Most of us are trying to live authentic lives, often learning from experience some of the large and small mistakes we believe our parents made raising us. Sometimes we have to unlearn a lot in order to discover who we truly are. I thrived when I was free to be myself, no longer under the spell of an autocratic mother. In order to be happy, we must learn to think for ourselves as well as to stand on our own two feet.

I've come to understand I am not here to judge; I am here to live, to grow, to accept what I cannot change, and to be courageous. As I mature, becoming inwardly aware, I find myself learning the lessons I need to know, often from painful situations that I have been exposed to. Some of these came in childhood. No parents are perfect. No mother can have a relationship with her children without some heartaches and significant differences of opinion. With my own daughters I embrace our differences as well as the things we share in common.

In order to live the truth as we see it, we often have to make critical choices to raise our own children entirely differently from the way we were brought up. I was afraid of my mother; my daughters are certainly not afraid of me. I tried to teach them right from wrong through example, not force. My mother gave me milk; I have tried to give Alexandra and Brooke milk and honey. Milk is our basic need; honey is the fun, the happiness, the joy.

In my desire to give my daughters honey, I raised them as though they were my grandchildren. They both went to good, strict private schools, where their teachers demanded a great deal from them. I tended to hug them, love them and reinforce their great qualities and strengths.

Today, my two daughters are my teachers, trusted friends, and the most precious relationship life has provided. When they are proud of me, I get jelly-legged because neither Alexandra nor Brooke is a pushover. They have high standards. They intuitively seem to know the true from the bogus. They sense what is right and what is not.

I feel grateful that early on I trusted that my daughters would thrive in an atmosphere of acceptance and love. It seemed clear to me that the Golden Rule works: I raised them singing their praises. And when their report cards came in the mail, I chose not to open them. As a gesture of trust and good faith, I put them on the front hall table for them to see when they got home from school. When they came to show me their good grades, I was proud of them. But there were good grades and bad grades; I always knew they were theirs, not mine. I respected their efforts to focus and achieve excellence in school. I never helped the girls with their homework. The school assigned work to the students, not the parents. I encouraged them. We discussed essay themes, but they handed in their own work.

Motherhood has taught me many things, and the role continues to evolve. I remember the day a teenaged Alexandra wore cobalt blue mascara to a football game and I asked her not to do so again. She was understandably furious. Years later we burst out in poignant laughter when she noticed I was wearing blue mascara with a new blue suit she had helped me pick out.

I was wrong. I've learned it is important to choose our battles, saving criticism for the really important issues. I did what felt right at the time. But I was awkward and often mistaken.

Some of the truths that are most important to me are things my daughters have learned over the course of their lives so far. They know the basics, to be sure. But as their mother, I often wonder if I couldn't tell them more. What things do I want to be certain they know for their safe and happy journey?

No one can tell anyone everything. Truth evolves and is relative, always discovered and rediscovered. However, in the course of thinking about how I can, in some way, help these wise daughters lead happier, healthier, and more productive and meaningful lives, I decided to write this book.

These "things" were gleaned from wisdom I have collected through reading great works and spending time with great people. While some of them are my own, you will recognize many other truths I think are treasures.

And although the book is dedicated to Alexandra and Brooke, I hope these insights will be helpful throughout your life and in the lives of your loved ones. I have learned these things, often the hard way, and wish that I had known them earlier.

I have developed a philosophy that enables me to live a very deep, exhilarating, complicated life with pleasure and happiness. I hope my insights inspire you and your loved ones to live a beautiful, satisfying life also.

HAPPINESS IS THE MEANING AND THE PURPOSE OF LIFE,
THE WHOLE AIM AND END OF HUMAN EXISTENCE.

Aristotle

Things I Want
My Daughters to Know

Find Work You Love That Supports You Financially

※

TO FIND OUT WHAT ONE IS FITTED TO DO,
AND TO SECURE AN OPPORTUNITY TO DO IT,
IS THE KEY TO HAPPINESS.

John Dewey

The work we choose to do each day accumulatively becomes our life's work. The opportunity to do good work stimulates our life force. My life has been shaped, enriched, and transformed by my love of my work. I work for life satisfaction. Through the happiest times in my life, as well as the most painful ones, my work has always sustained me.

The world doesn't owe us anything. We owe everything to the world. Our work is our way of expressing ourselves, of being a cocreator in this dynamic earthly journey we call life. You decide what your work is, and your work may be much larger than your "job." Try to envision the big picture as you move along.

Through our work we give back to the world a portion of what we've been given. Our reward emerges from the work itself. We work to grow, to stretch ourselves, to discover new truths, to deepen, and to serve. We become more aware and more alive when we find work that we believe is important and that we love doing. We transcend ourselves through work that makes us discover more about what we really believe in and what we truly love to do.

Through our work we're given opportunities to reconsider our thinking. In my career as a decorator, I was trained to create formal rooms based on eighteenth-century aesthetics. Through experience and exposure, I realized I enjoyed a more relaxed, informal style for living. It became my mission to help clients create homes that reflected their unique personal style and needs. This mission eventually led to my current career as an author and speaker on living beautifully. Thus our work expands our personal potential; we're rewarded with a greater understanding of what is true for us and what our contributions can be.

Why am I so happy that my work is always available to me? I am self-employed. I am a self-starter. I can prepare a lecture or seminar. I can write. I can decorate or sell art. Whatever I do, I enjoy the process. I am a student of life, of truth. I study the classics in the interstices of the day. I carry a tote bag with me when I travel so I can read, write in notebooks, and continue to learn.

When you find work you love that supports you financially, that is ideal. Hundreds of people have confided in me that when they do work they love—as a teacher or a librarian, a yoga instructor, a college advisor or a dancer—they don't need as much money because they are happy. When people are not happy in their work, they have a tendency to want more money because they are unfulfilled by their work.

If you don't love your work, but it puts food on the table and provides for you and your loved ones, this is not ideal; but working to survive is honorable. An actress waits on tables at a restaurant while she auditions for roles. Temporarily, this is fine; you do what you have to do to live. This shouldn't be the case indefinitely, because it can be draining, sapping your vitality and enthusiasm, and selling your soul. This is not your true work; it is a paying job. If you must do this, enrich the rest of your life by seeking out activities that will feed your soul.

What would be ideal work for you? What are you doing to move toward this goal? What if you find work that fulfills your monetary needs and involves you to some degree, but is not wholly satisfying? What then? Try to enjoy fully the parts of it you can and satisfy other interests through volunteering, hobbies, and spending time with your family. Your untapped skills may be put to good use through volunteer work that may enrich you nontangibly.

Stay in touch with your feelings. You can't afford to become bitter because your job isn't what you hoped it would be. Keep striving for work that really fits the big picture. Aim high. A key to a happy, well-lived life is to find work you love that allows you financial independence.

Don't settle forever, or for too long, for work you don't love. You need to aspire to work that makes you thrive, that you're proud of, that is a perfect fit to your talents, gifts, and passionate interests. In order to use our energy constructively, we need to pursue work we love. When we love our work, we will sustain true, inner happiness. Work and love, love and work, become one.

When we love our work, we become energized by it, not enervated. Seek and find work that allows you to give your gifts to the universe as you teach yourself new skills. We shouldn't merely work for a living: we should work to make a life. Work can be what leads us to help our community or our world, and to produce something lasting. For a blessed few, history has shown us, work can bring immortality.

No matter what happens to you, when you love your work, you will maintain your independence and, therefore, your freedom. As an adult, finding work you love is your responsibility and, I believe, your duty. If you find it, it promises to bring harmony to the rest of your life. We're here to develop our gifts, to share them with others in service. The ideal is to find paid work that nourishes you and others. Loving our work is primary to accomplishing this goal.

> WHERE YOUR PLEASURE IS, THERE IS YOUR TREASURE;
> WHERE YOUR TREASURE, THERE YOUR HEART;
> WHERE YOUR HEART, THERE YOUR HAPPINESS.
>
> *Saint Augustine*

It's Easier to Get into Things Than It Is to Get Out of Them

❋

We tend to go through life saying to others, yes, yes, yes—while saying to ourselves, oops, oops, oops. Looking ahead, we think we're doing the right, decent thing. Looking back, we realize we didn't know enough about the consequences of our agreement. A project can look intriguing when we agree to take it on, but if we discover it is wrong for us, we may stand to lose everything. Often the only choice we really have is to walk sadly away empty-handed.

Learn to anticipate when saying yes goes against your best interests. I once told my husband, Peter, a year in advance that I would host a dinner party at our apartment for one of his organizations. Soon afterwards I received an invitation to speak in San Francisco on the same date. Neither function could be rescheduled, and I had a defining moment when I realized that my career had to take priority over being a hostess. I let Peter down and went to California to give the talk. He had a cocktail reception at the apartment before he and the guests all went to a favorite neighborhood restaurant for dinner. I said yes but changed my mind under changed circumstances. Don't rush into projects and commitments until you reflect on the probable consequences. Stay focused on your own priorities and responsibilities.

When asked to attend social events, knowing my private family time and professional work are my top priorities, I now say, "I'll try." Try not to promise anything unless you're willing to see it through. And if you postpone or have to renege on something you have agreed to, be prepared to make it up to the other person another time.

Whether it's family traditions, regular meetings with a friend, or volunteering your time, making a clean break is often difficult. Be careful not to have a set date to run with a friend three times a week. You should be free to let the spirit move you—to go for a run alone or with the dog—without embarrassment or apologies.

Don't allow yourself to be drawn into battles you don't want to fight. If you have an argument with a family member, friend, spouse, or coworker over a silly misunderstanding, politely excuse yourself and walk away. Spend some time alone to regain your inner peace. Don't go back until you are beyond embellishing things, bringing up the past, or saying things you don't mean that you'll later regret.

There are times when we think we know enough to make a serious life-changing commitment, only to discover how uninformed we really were. When we're young, we think a marriage is the wedding, the wardrobe, the presents, the parties, and the honeymoon. Then, as the days, months, and years pass, we may find the reality of our choice is all wrong for us. Many people stay in an empty marriage because they are too afraid or embarrassed to break the legal contract and to divorce.

Be careful. Be aware. It's easier to get into things than it is to get out of them. Use your good judgment.

EVERYONE COMPLAINS OF HIS MEMORY,
BUT NO ONE COMPLAINS OF HIS JUDGMENT.

La Rochefoucauld

Think Positively:
You Will Live Longer Than a Pessimist

❋

PAINT THE WALLS OF YOUR MIND WITH MANY BEAUTIFUL PICTURES.

William Lyon Phelps

You are the only one who chooses what you think. Think the thoughts that will increase your sense of well-being. Think the thoughts that make you feel good. We become what we think about all day. Positive thinkers stay connected to their creative power and use all their powers constructively, staying focused on what they want to accomplish and how they want to feel, doing the best they can to look for the good in every situation. Negative thinkers find themselves feeling scattered. Negative thoughts prey harmfully on us, triggering a number of distinctive emotions: anger, confusion, anxiety, depression, and frustration. Negative emotion appears to weaken people's immune system. Psychology, indeed, does affect biology.

Look up "negative" in any dictionary and you will clearly see that negativity is destructive and dangerous to your health and hope for happiness. Thinking negatively is not a characteristic that is deemed positive, affirmative, or desirable. Negative thinkers have a tendency to be gloomy and pessimistic and to have an unfavorable outlook. They lack the flexibility of constructive thinking, instead creating opposition or resistance to a situation's solution.

A few years after Peter and I were married, while on an island vacation, we met with a classmate of Peter's and his wife to play tennis. I'd stopped playing competitively; this was meant to be a friendly, social, mixed-doubles game. We rapidly found ourselves being trounced by our opponents. Going back to the fence to retrieve some balls, Peter and I smiled. We were behind 0–6, 0–5. It was my serve. Peter winked and whispered positively, "Let's whip them." We won that set 7–5 and the next 6–0, winning the match. Not only did I win my serve, but we broke their serves. We played the game to win. In tennis, when you want to win, you have to envision yourself having won. When you're pinned against a wall, losing every point, a negative attitude can cause double faults, careless errors, and lack of courage. Our choice to think positively was powerful, freeing us to be more effective and to win the match.

Failure can make us vulnerable to negative thinking. None of us likes rejection. After several years of work on a manuscript for a book about happiness, I admitted to myself that my approach was too scientific, too impersonal, and too technical. I had attacked the researchers for not focusing on what's right about us, for their emphasis on misery and pathology. This didn't make for positive reading, even though I felt strongly about it. Then I swung the opposite way and wrote the book from a spiritual perspective. When I submitted my manuscript to the publisher, I was not only positive, I was sure they would embrace it. Alas, they said it was "unpublishable."

After all those years of intense effort and hard work, I felt I'd wasted my time. I went for a walk to Stonington Point, where I love to watch boats come and go from the harbor. I sat on a favorite rock perch and cried as the mist and spray from the water merged with my tears. I was left with nothing concrete to show for all my research, study, and insights. Two manuscripts that didn't work out. What went wrong?

Mesmerized by the solitude, slowly absorbing the shock and disappointment, I came to understand that my goal was to make my book about happiness publishable. I returned to the cottage determined to find a solution. I could not quit. I didn't push against what was not "working." We are all more effective when we "don't fight the problem." With good advice and deep thought I focused on my goal to have this body of work published. It was, and successfully.

In order to get the most out of your lifetime, formulate a positive philosophy and search, not for the ideal later, but for the actual good now. You must have a point of view, a perspective, on life. You always have a choice to select the window you look out from. Choose the best possible view. Look for ways to expand your horizon and multiply your possibilities. Choose to look at life from a sense of increase, a sense of potential. Being positive is being appreciative of the miracle of your life, even when things are not going your way. A positive attitude looks for progress, ways to improve things and make things work out for the best.

I'm grateful to the fourteenth-century mystic Julian of Norwich, the first female writer to be published in English, who reassured us that we are taken care of by a power greater than ourselves:

> *I shall make all things well,*
> *and I will make all things well;*
> *and you will see yourself that every*
> *kind of thing will be well.*

All is well. Well-being is our natural state. There is far more good than bad in the world, more beauty than ugliness, more kindness than meanness, more love than hate.

Can we make a distinction between positive thinking and Pollyannaism, where people are foolishly or blindly optimistic? I believe that being positive in all situations is always appropriate, but be realistic about being positive. Avoid sugarcoated truths. The actual truth of things is the prize. Face it. If there is some good you can do in a serious situation, do it. If not, accept it. Don't get mired in a negative frame of mind that is a dead-end bust. You can choose to cultivate your character to respond nobly in all situations. Being positive is a habit to be developed that then becomes the bedrock of your authenticity.

Some people think that worrying is a kind of preventive action. I worried when I was younger, when I had little self-confidence as a parent and had big responsibilities. Worrying didn't help me to succeed; my skills, intelligence, and effort did. When we worry, we feel a nagging concern, an uneasiness. We become troubled and anxious. We brood. Negative thought can be counterproductive and lead nowhere. I've cultivated a positive mental state of living in the present moment. Through mindfulness training, meditation, and breathing techniques, people can learn not to worry.

When you find yourself in a situation that makes you feel uneasy, ask yourself, "What is the worst thing that could happen in this situation? What can I do to make the situation better?" Ask yourself, "Have I done anything wrong?" If you have, how can you correct things? Are you doing your best? Are you trying to think positively about the situation? Do you feel you are worrying about something that is very unlikely to happen?

To overcome a tendency to worry, start with simple actions to support your positive energy. Select a healthy, balanced diet. Don't eat too much. Get adequate sleep. If you are going through a rough patch, try to get some extra sleep. Whenever we are exhausted, we tend to be more negative than positive, looking at the glass as half empty rather than half full. Worry is exacerbated by exhaustion and stress.

Excessive worry and stress can be harnessed by positive emotions. When you find your thoughts are negative, think of one positive thought and stick with it, with no interference, for seventeen seconds.

Look at the second hand of your watch to time yourself. If you achieve this, studies indicate that the positive energy will be registered in your consciousness. Build on this.

I know empirically that this is a well-ordered universe. There are principles that never fail. There is danger in thinking negative thoughts— negative results will always follow. You don't prevent problems from happening by dwelling on negative thoughts; rather, you may be creating them because of your lack of faith and belief in a good solution. If you look for beauty, you'll see it in an onion, an egg, a dandelion, a soap bubble, a raindrop, a snowflake, or a ray of light. If we look for the bad, our eyes can find it—at a garbage dump, in graffiti, in scenes of war or terrorism, or the sight of a parent hitting a child.

Ask yourself what thoughts increase your vitality, elevate your mood, uplift your spirits, and bring you closer toward enlightenment. Think the thoughts that will create a deepened life experience. Positive thoughts can become habit, our new way of thinking. Learn to resist outside experiences that interrupt your pure flow of positive energy.

Positive thinking, I believe, is essential to radiant health. But beyond the fact that we optimists will live nineteen percent longer than pessimists, we will be living in the light, in joy, not in darkness.

Look up toward the sky. Immediately you will feel better physiologically. The sky is infinite light. You are here to add to your own light.

Criteria of Emotional Maturity

❋ THE ABILITY TO DEAL CONSTRUCTIVELY WITH REALITY . . .

❋ THE CAPACITY TO ADAPT TO CHANGE . . .

❋ THE CAPACITY TO FIND MORE SATISFACTION
IN GIVING THAN RECEIVING . . .

❋ THE CAPACITY TO LOVE

William C. Menninger, MD

In Really Tough Times, Regularly Take Time Off

❁

WHEN THE WORLD IS STORM-DRIVEN AND THE BAD THAT HAPPENS
AND THE WORSE THAT THREATENS ARE SO URGENT AS TO SHUT OUT
EVERYTHING ELSE FROM VIEW, THEN WE NEED TO KNOW ALL
THE STRONG FORTRESSES OF THE SPIRIT.

Edith Hamilton

When you are in a crisis, you focus all your energy toward the situation at hand. You're there all the way. However, caregivers can't continue to take care unless they replenish their own well.

If we don't take care of ourselves in anxious situations, we deplete our energy, ultimately making it impossible for us to be helpful. As painful as it is, walk away from the hospital room, sickbed, or place where you are a vital caregiver as soon as someone arrives to cover for you. Remind yourself that your soul needs you too; you can't give more to others than you have.

I've learned that the more traumatic and emotionally stressful a situation is, the more I need to regularly remove myself in order to remain positive, optimistic, cheerful, and healthy. When we are the cheerleaders, we root with all our strength. We can't let ourselves get swallowed up in the routine of illness and emergency without breaks. We have to be the inspiration for someone who is struggling to become well. This requires all of our inner resources. Value the vital role you are playing in these difficult times. Keep your spirits uplifted. A loved one is in great need of you.

In the case of terminal illness and death, the fuller your heart is with love, the more comfort and positive feeling you will transfer to the one who is soon to die.

Pace yourself. You never know how long a tough time is going to last. Because tough times bring family and friends together, there is almost always a support team in place to help you temporarily leave the scene. Don't spend that away time with a friend or family member. Be alone and be free. Go for a walk. Read an inspirational book you carry with you. Get a massage. Window-shop. Savor an ice cream cone. Buy some flowers. Go to a coffee shop. Go where you'll hear the laughter of children and can see dogs wagging their tails. Seek the healing therapy of light however and wherever possible.

Nothing lasts. Everything will be different soon. Give yourself fully to the difficult times in your life. When you are giving one hundred percent emotionally and spiritually, keep yourself uplifted, fresh, and cheerful.

When my mother was dying, I went from the hospital in Connecticut where she was a patient to San Diego to give a lecture. Mother taped the brochure to the wall near her bed; she was so proud of me. I needed to take that time off, to be with healthy people, to be myself, to tend to my life. She needed to know her daughter was out there, fulfilling a vital role.

After Peter's emergency knee surgery, I spent all day at the hospital but treasured the opportunity to kiss him good-bye and go to a nearby restaurant with Brooke for a break. This was so important. Days later, after four nights of sleeping on the hospital room floor, I went home, bathed, washed my hair, and slept for several hours in our bed. I returned with fresh clothes and some books and magazines, restored by the beauty and colors in our home. My time off also helped me decide that Peter would heal faster and better at home than in a rehabilitation hospital. I was right. My time off paid off.

THE WORLD IN WHICH YOU LIVE IS NOT PRIMARILY DETERMINED
BY OUTWARD CONDITIONS AND CIRCUMSTANCES
BUT BY THE THOUGHTS THAT HABITUALLY OCCUPY YOUR MIND.

Norman Vincent Peale

Don't Lay Down a Law with a Child That You Are Not Prepared to Enforce

❋

HYPOCRISY, THE ONLY EVIL THAT WALKS INVISIBLE.

John Milton

Discipline strengthens children. You give out cookies here and there, but setting certain rules for your child to obey helps to build his or her confidence. At the same time, you shouldn't make up rules arbitrarily. We must be prepared to stick with the ones we do have so that the child respects that although our rules are few, they are rules that really matter.

I raised my daughters assuming the best of them. Rarely did I need to discipline them. They disciplined themselves for the most part. But when they broke a rule, I stuck to my guns. I always enforced a rule, as painful as it was to do so.

The rules you set should teach your children self-respect as well as self-control. I let my daughters help establish the rules so they were in agreement with our family policies and considered them fair and reasonable. We would talk things out until we all agreed. We often changed a curfew to fit the occasion but were strict about adhering to the agreed-upon time.

Teach your children how to have fun, how to be happy, and how to help others. They will echo your example. When they're toddlers, enjoy teaching them new words and colors, playing with them in the park, teaching them about all of the different animals in the zoo, going to bookstores, playing in the sandbox, having a picnic including some of their favorite treats, taking them with you on errands. Everything is exciting to toddlers. When you do your grocery shopping, they point out what *"num-nums"* they love. While taking the dog for a walk with you, your toddler is exposed to beauty. A pebble is a diamond; a stick is a magic wand.

In the school years, listen as your children enthusiastically show and tell. They want to share what they're learning, what is exciting them. Be there to receive these precious gifts. The teenage years are the beginning of the process of separation. They want to be with you less and with their friends more. Get to know their friends. Treat them to meals at some of their favorite restaurants. Have your home be the place they all want to be. Popcorn and soft drinks work wonders. The more your children's friends enjoy you, the less your children will be mortified by what you say, what you wear, or what you do.

Humor is key to keeping the family energy positive, especially with teenagers. Laugh together at life's ironies. Laughter always clears the air. No one remembers the mediocre, the ho-hum, the bland or ordinary. The more enjoyable time you spend together, the better. Whether you go on a fishing trip or a shopping trip for school clothes, these are opportunities, when they are away from their friends, to let your children into your intimate world. Tell stories. Show them your passions. Indulge in your favorite ice cream cone, skip, dance, and laugh at yourself.

When someone is in need, let your children help out with making get-well cards, cookies, or soup, or paying a visit to cheer someone up. Happiness is always true when we are adding to the happiness of others. Through your own generosity of spirit, you show your children how to happily spread their joy around them.

Children thrive when they are understood and loved, and given the time and attention of their parents. Think positively about every stage of your children's development. They will spread their wings and test their boundaries. This is how they learn and grow toward self-mastery.

Let them know that you expect them to be trustworthy. Then trust them. Don't assume the worst or accuse before you know the facts. Rules are created to limit behavior. Have only important rules. How do you judge what are important ones? How do you make the punishment fit the violation? You determine what important rules are from your own experience. They change under changed circumstances. Safety is a key issue. One rule at our house was that our children always had to tell us where they were going to be. If their plans changed, they let us know. We made it clear that they could and should bring a friend home to spend the night rather than drive with someone who had had too much to drink.

Let your children see how you work hard and play hard. Life is not one endless list of chores to be crossed off a list. Life is a celebration to be cherished in every stage. Stay alert to the privilege of being a parent, of being in their stimulating company, of being able to teach them through your continuous, steady example of love, fairness, kindness, and caring. When you believe your children are wonderful, they will be.

Your children are not just your children; they are children of the universe. Enjoy them.

EVERY GENERATION FINDS IT HARD TO HEAR WHAT ITS CHILDREN NEED—BECAUSE ITS CHILDHOOD IS STILL RINGING IN ITS EARS.

Ellen Goodman

Travel Heavy

❁

CONSIDERING LIFE'S BREVITY, WE SHOULD TRAVEL ABUNDANTLY,
WITH GREAT ENTHUSIASM.

Peter Megargee Brown

When the late and talented interior designer Mark Hampton went to graduate school, he brought steamer trunks full of treasured objects, decorative boxes, obelisks, flowers, books, music, and candles. When his new roommate arrived later on, Mark was on the floor styling the room. "Hi, I'm Mark. I travel heavy," he said.

When I went to Paris on my honeymoon, I brought all the clothes I loved. It was more than I needed, to be sure. But you never know what the weather will be like or what will suit your mood.

I realize sages advise us not to be burdened by baggage. But I love things. And I love to travel. Whenever I travel lightly, I regret it. On a recent trip with Peter, I packed lightly, just enough for five days and nights. Optimistically hoping for abundant sunshine and warm evenings, we arrived to freezing, wind-chilling rain. I had to immediately rush out with a borrowed umbrella in a storm to shop for foul-weather gear, instead of enjoying a museum or a café. I ended up overpaying for drab, ugly windbreakers with hoods that we literally lived in the whole time. How much more comfortable and in the swing of things we'd have felt —and more chic—if we'd had our familiar rain gear.

You will be happiest when you are prepared. Bring with you whatever you envision you might need. When I traveled with my Aunt Betty around the world as a teenager in 1959, staying in youth hostels, I brought along a camera, film, books, notebooks, sketchpads, journals, pens, and a baby pillow for emotional comfort. To this day I enjoy bringing whatever I need in order to work when I'm away from home. I always travel with a paperback dictionary. I bring scarves, jewelry, a travel clock, a bathing suit, a raincoat, and an umbrella. I have a small amount of the currency of the country before I arrive. (Just getting a luggage cart at an airport requires a coin.) Being self-sufficient in a strange place is empowering. Traveling heavy reduces anxiety.

Travel heavy to live big, significant lives. Have a stimulating career. Have children. Have a dog. Have plants you need to water. Have a personal library. Have dinner parties. Collect inanimate objects simply because you love them.

The beauty you surround yourself with enriches your soul. I'm here on this planet for a fleeting time. I have no interest in renouncing material pleasures. You can't take your temporary possessions with you when you take your last breath. Now is the only time to enjoy these possessions that make you happy now.

You will never regret traveling heavy.

IF WE ARE BASICALLY POSITIVE IN ATTITUDE . . . WE WILL ATTRACT
AND CREATE PEOPLE, SITUATIONS, AND EVENTS WHICH CONFORM
TO OUR POSITIVE EXPECTATIONS.

Shakti Gawain

You Don't Have to Prove Anything to Anyone

❋

WISE MEN EMBRACE THE ONE
AND SET AN EXAMPLE TO ALL.
NOT PUTTING ON A DISPLAY,
THEY SHINE FORTH.
NOT JUSTIFYING THEMSELVES,
THEY ARE DISTINGUISHED.
NOT BOASTING,
THEY RECEIVE RECOGNITION.
NOT BRAGGING,
THEY NEVER FALTER.

Lao Tsu

Please yourself. Learn to forgive yourself. Continue to build your self-confidence and your self-love by looking at how far you've come, and what you have overcome. You're evolving; you're becoming a more intuitive, productive person.

I often say, "I don't know," when someone asks me a serious question. We don't have to have the answers. If there is an ultimate truth, we don't always know what it is.

Whatever your beliefs are, you do not have to justify them to others.

Do you believe in evil? Do you believe in angels? Do you believe in hell? Do you believe in life after death? Do you believe in original sin? Do you believe in your own divinity? Do you believe that animals have souls? Do you believe in happiness? Yes, no, and maybe?

Some people become so opinionated about their beliefs that they are willing to die for them—or have someone else die for them. Others are on a quest for truth that totally absorbs them, questioning their former beliefs, stretching their minds to new dimensions of insights. When you are interested in the meaning of life, in finding fulfillment, in finding significance in what you think, feel, and do, you can live authentically, but it is not your job to reform others. If someone doesn't ask your opinion, it is better not to offer it. If someone asks my advice, I often say, "What do you think?" They need to be encouraged to use their inner resources and inquiry. We can be extremely useful to others by encouraging them to go inside themselves and tap into their own guidance system that is always there to inform them.

Don't try to prove anything about yourself to anyone. It isn't necessary. Your worth shines through to others—know your worth.

Can you remember a time when you tried to prove something to someone and realized it was pointless? I remember a time in my early twenties when I successfully resisted the impulse to do so, and kept my dignity. I was traveling in a car with my former mother-in-law, who told me how selfish I was not to begin a family. "There is never a convenient time. There is never enough money. You shouldn't think of your career. You are married now. You should get pregnant and have a baby." As she drove along the coast road in Connecticut, I enjoyed watching the waves lap onto the sandy shores. I worked on my breathing. Deep breaths in. I bit my lower lip until it bled. I'd endured over a dozen excruciating procedures, was in the hands of a well-respected fertility expert, and had experienced the loss of a miscarriage. What was there to prove? I remained silent, holding back tears.

I remember inviting my in-laws to lunch at the cottage. After serving iced tea and cheese sticks, Peter and I invited everyone to wash hands. We were off to have lobster salad at a dock a few hundred yards away. My sister-in-law was seething ("We drove two hours to have lunch with you and you didn't bother to cook for us? You didn't care enough to make any effort at all?"). I could tell she was furious. We sipped iced tea out of plastic cups with straws (not cut crystal). We ate fresh, delicious lobster salad while looking at the boats in the harbor. We were enjoying a summer's afternoon in fresh air, on the water. How great is that? I let it go. I talked about the weather. There's just no point in telling someone to loosen up and enjoy the moment in the sun.

When I was working at the firm of my mentor, Mrs. Brown, at the firm word got out that I'd written a decorating book. At that time, I had a superior at the firm who felt she had the right to read and critique my book prior to publication. "After all, Sandie, you are representing the firm. You must let me read it." Knowing what a trap that was, I calmly told her I was not representing the firm; I had written a book that reflected my point of view about decorating. I dedicated it to Mrs. Archibald Manning Brown, my mentor. The flap copy simply read, "Alexandra Stoddard has been associated with the interior design firm of McMillen, Inc., for twelve years." When I was invited to be on the *Today* show with Barbara Walters, I was also invited to have a publication party at this colleague's apartment.

You are vastly different from your parents, relatives, friends, and acquaintances. Maintain a sense of privacy and an inner world. You know you can never conform to others' expectations. We spend most of our lives trying to unlearn much of what we've been taught. We can't inherit a philosophy; we can't pretend we think and feel as others do.

I'm unself-conscious about the opinion others have of me as long as I am being true to myself. Whenever I alter my behavior to try to fit in more, I know I am off my path. There is no way you can live authentically and simultaneously worry about what others think of the way you dress, the choices you make, the way you value your time. You are the only person you can completely please. When you are honest with yourself, you have something wonderful to offer to others, always on your terms.

Don't expose yourself to criticism from people who are not able to understand your complexity. Your personal responsibility is to be yourself, to remain true to yourself. You never have to prove anything to anyone.

WHAT A MAN THINKS OF HIMSELF, THAT IS WHAT DETERMINES,
OR RATHER, INDICATES, HIS FATE.

Henry David Thoreau

An Invitation Is Not an Obligation

❊

WHAT LIES IN OUR POWER TO DO, IT LIES IN OUR POWER NOT TO DO.

Aristotle

An invitation is a request—the act of asking for your presence and participation—not a command performance. We are flattered to think someone would want to include us on his or her guest list. To go or not to go: how do you decide?

Invitations are for a future event at a specific time and place. They're often for a special occasion—a graduation, a wedding, an engagement party, a baby shower, a housewarming, a fund-raiser, or a gathering to honor someone. Every invitation has to be weighed to be sure you accept the ones you truly want to attend, and decline the ones that are not a good fit for you at the time.

We all have different amounts of time, energy, and money. Carefully weigh whether an invitation is appropriate for you. Think of yourself first. Do you want to go? Will it be fun? Do you know some of the people who will be there? Do you have to travel far to get there and back? Do you have clothes you like that you can wear or will it require buying a new outfit? How much is it going to cost you in time, energy, and money if you RSVP yes?

When it comes to invitations, there are only three words worth knowing: yes, no, and wow. I've been invited to thrilling parties I'll never forget. I've also made a big effort to go to some parties where I wished I had stayed home and read.

If an event sounds good, is nearby, and you can go conveniently, this could qualify for yes. But some occasions are inconvenient to get to and may not be that meaningful to you. Think things through in order not to waste your precious time and resources.

If you say no, say it nicely. Send a written note of thanks; this will take you five minutes and cost you a stamp. Saying yes to a wedding that you'd rather not attend could cost you thirty-seven hours and hundreds of dollars.

Show up whenever you can for your dearest friends' events no matter how much trouble it is. When you can't, for whatever reasons, remember you can't be all things to all people and have a life. Do not feel pressured into doing something against your will. Never feel an ounce of guilt for saying no politely. Your real friends will give you your space. When your heart is in the right place, be confident you've done the right thing.

Where should you go? Whom should you spend time with? Why? Be honestly selective. What you don't do is often as important as what you do.

TO LIVE CONTENT WITH SMALL MEANS; TO SEEK ELEGANCE
RATHER THAN LUXURY, AND REFINEMENT RATHER THAN FASHION;
TO BE WORTHY, NOT RESPECTABLE, AND WEALTHY, NOT RICH;
TO STUDY HARD, THINK QUIETLY, TALK GENTLY, ACT FRANKLY;
TO LISTEN TO STARS AND BIRDS, TO BABES AND SAGES,
WITH OPEN HEART; TO BEAR ALL CHEERFULLY, DO ALL BRAVELY,
AWAIT OCCASIONS, HURRY NEVER. IN A WORD,
TO LET THE SPIRITUAL, UNBIDDEN AND UNCONSCIOUS, GROW UP
THROUGH THE COMMON. THIS IS TO BE MY SYMPHONY.

William Henry Channing

Be Grateful but Don't Expect Gratitude

※

BLESSED IS HE WHO EXPECTS NO GRATITUDE,
FOR HE SHALL NOT BE DISAPPOINTED.

William Bennett

I wrote an essay in second grade entitled, "Being Greatful." I misspelled *grateful* and was reprimanded, but I now believe we become great in proportion to how grateful we are. You receive vitality and comfort every time you are grateful.

When your natural attitude is of pleasure in being grateful, you look upon your life as a precious gift. Everything comes as a blessing. Have a receptive, grateful heart. Try not to take anything or anyone for granted. Do for others because you want to, not because they will be thankful. Even doing something for a loved one will not necessarily bring gratitude in return.

I'd rather be loved than thanked. When we expect others to appreciate everything we do, we set ourselves up for disappointment. There are thousands of little things we do to make ourselves and others happy. People are not necessarily taking us for granted because they don't recognize every detail of our effort to make their lives run smoothly.

Whatever you do, do it with love and a pure heart. You do what you do to enrich your life. You want to do the right thing at the right time for the right reasons because it is the good thing to do.

You may think that you are getting drawn into thankless jobs by others, but you can turn the situation around by your sense of self-appreciation. Learn to appreciate your own efforts and sense of caring. If you lower your expectations of endless thanks, you allow for high satisfaction. Do your best in every situation not because you want praise or gratitude, but because doing less would be out of character. Do what needs to be done. Appreciate yourself. You know what you're doing. Wanting to be appreciated is human, but you are also divine. Be grateful for this truth.

When you give a dinner party, don't wait for a thank-you note. When you send a gift, don't expect a letter of thanks. Loved ones will forget your birthday; don't dwell on it. If you are upset because of other people's lack of appreciation, it means you have more work to do on yourself. Look into your heart. Should you examine your motives for doing too much for others?

If you overpromise and take on too much caretaking, ask yourself why you are taking on something that is beyond your capacity to perform in a caring, kind, loving way. Stay in touch with your feelings. If your life is out of balance and you feel resentment, anger, or become depressed, stop doing what you're doing; you are feeling sorry for yourself. When you do something for someone in an attitude of self-pity, you are not being helpful.

We don't undertake the hard work of raising children to be thanked. Being a parent teaches us the miracle of having a child born through us, but not from us. We are here to help children become free, self-reliant, and independent. When we do our job as parents, our children leave the nest and live their own unique lives. We're grateful for the sacred opportunity to have them look up to us, love us, honor us, spend their childhood with us. We're grateful we were there for their first steps, their first love, their birthdays, and their graduations. Be grateful for this incredible privilege of witnessing and facilitating their life's passage. Children shouldn't be forced to say thank you. When you have children, it's all about them, not you. This is how it should be.

Love your children unconditionally and do your best to understand them. Don't clip their wings by insisting on gratitude. Be grateful they're able to fly so high.

I BELIEVE THAT UNARMED TRUTH AND UNCONDITIONAL LOVE
WILL HAVE THE FINAL WORD IN REALITY.

Martin Luther King, Jr.

Pain Is Inevitable; Suffering Is a Choice

THERE IS NO COMING TO CONSCIOUSNESS WITHOUT PAIN.

Carl Jung

Loss is a major theme in life. We should be preparing ourselves for it every day. As the psychologist and teacher William James suggested, we should take things gently. Look for the little good every day as if life were to last a hundred years. This habit will help sustain you in sad times.

I believe in healing, not grieving. We must try to discipline ourselves to accept what we can't change and move on. Suffering can be overcome when it is transformed into healing and growth. We go deeper. What you have at this moment will never return to you. By living mindfully, you fully value the present, not taking anything for granted. What you have now may be the best there can be.

Consider the losses that may cause you to be deprived of something or someone. You could lose a loved one through death. You could lose your health. Your house could be destroyed by flood or fire. You could lose your job, income, and professional standing. You could have an accident and lose your ability to walk. You could lose your art or jewelry by theft.

We can't cling too tightly to what we have, but we can appreciate the people and things we love. Cultivate a stronger affection for what you have right now in your life. Be grateful for the privilege of being able to love so abundantly. When you meditate on all that you have that provides you with a magnificent life, you will gracefully be able to accept losses as they come.

Fully enjoy your newborn baby. When you wake up one morning and this innocent child has become a rambunctious toddler, you shed a tear that you no longer have a baby. This is only the first stage in the ongoing evolution of growth, independence, and freedom.

Try to experience life with a view from the top, so that you can see the full picture in all its wonderful detail. Rather than focusing on what looks bleak, practice looking through the eyes of the "opulent good." When a child smiles at you, this is good. When your spouse walks up behind you and rubs your shoulders as you sit at your desk, this is good. When you see a beautiful sunrise, you are glad you are alive for one more day. Breathe in life's goodness. Don't take anything for granted. Even in the midst of loss, we can realize just how sacred and beautiful our lives are. Love never takes anything away completely. All things change and are transformed. The little good is always present when we look for it.

When you experience loss, forgive those who cry, say the wrong thing, or have such negative energy that they are a challenge to your healing. Society, religion, family, and friends have awkward ways of trying to support us in our painful hours. Everyone tends to become so dreary and dark. Pity is never appropriate. I don't believe in excess sympathy. Love, empathy, and compassion are always appreciated, always timely. Have strategies in place to deflect well-meant but misguided efforts. You don't need to be reminded of how awful the loss is. You're in a stage of reconstruction, of taking all the threads of your life and weaving a fresh new tapestry. Feel free to walk away. Be sure you get lots of sleep. Don't see people for long visits. When you're with others, do something active, something uplifting. Go to a museum or to a tea-house or on an outing in the car. When you're at home with family and friends, bake biscuits or brownies. Arrange flowers. Polish silver. Play favorite music. Have your children near you; they know how to make you laugh and smile through your tears. Be understanding of yourself and others. Everyone hurts in different ways for different reasons. Because you know what you'd like from others in your hours of pain, help them to heal also. Loss is loss to all of us.

We've been taught to suffer, to hold on to our pain. Try not to be overwhelmed by others, and trust that time will heal your pain. Whether you feel pain mentally or physically or spiritually, step back. Look at the big picture. Examine your emotions and what is actually causing you pain. Is it truly pain from a loss or breakup or terrible event, or is it anxiety related to someone or something surrounding what happened?

Maybe you didn't really know how sick your mother was before her sudden death. Were you in denial? Were there signals you didn't catch? Or you may feel guilty because you feel that you could have done more for someone you have now lost. Is there a financial concern? There are always issues that may not be resolved, but loss brings them into focus.

Identify the cause of the pain. Don't resist it or fight it. Work hard to understand what happened so you can start the healing process. We can try to face pain with grace and calmness knowing we are one with all that is. This brings a great sense of peace in experiencing life's events. What can you do for yourself and others? Try to live as normal a life as you can while you are living through a painful time. Learn from the loss, but don't dwell on it. Life shouldn't be defined by pain. There is whole-ness waiting to be born. Give birth to the healing process.

In times of your greatest pain, you should be with people who will make you laugh. Laughter, as we learned from Norman Cousins in his excellent book, *Anatomy of an Illness,* distracts us from pain, allowing healing to work its miracles. Cousins believed that hospitals were no place for sick people. He left the hospital, checked into a hotel, took himself off all medication, and laughed himself back to vibrant health.

Misfortune and challenges always teach us helpful lessons about ourselves. This is how we come to know our virtues and ourselves. Be kind to yourself. Do the things that make you feel better.

MAN WAS MADE FOR JOY AND WOE,
AND WHEN THIS WE RIGHTLY KNOW
THROUGH THE WORLD WE SAFELY GO.

William Blake

Be More a Generalist Than a Specialist

❀

HAVE A VARIETY OF INTERESTS. . . . THESE INTERESTS RELAX THE MIND
AND LESSEN TENSION ON THE NERVOUS SYSTEM. PEOPLE WITH MANY
INTERESTS LIVE, NOT ONLY LONGEST, BUT HAPPIEST.

George Matthew Allen

There is something to be said for being a jack-of-all-trades, even if you are also a master of one. Knowing a little about a lot of things that interest you adds to the richness of a whole, well-lived life.

Society pushes us to specialize, to become experts. This requires dedication to a particular occupation, branch of study or research—a narrow lens to look through. The drawback to being specialists is we often come to know more and more about less and less. There is a great deal of pressure to master one's field better than the competition. You may pursue training, degrees, or increasing levels of responsibility at work. Then you discover the pressure of having to keep up.

Some people seem willing to work around the clock in their narrow specialty. But such dedication can also diminish a sense of freedom. You could work at the office until ten each night, then look back and realize you would have loved to have gone home and enjoyed the sweetness of your family and friends, or traveled to far-off lands, exotic places, meeting interesting people. Johnny-one-note is indeed poor. Mastering one thing to the exclusion of others can tax and inhibit your true spirit.

We have only so much energy and time. Balance is key. Generalists view and contemplate the whole with all its connections. When you are in need of a specialist, you're always in a position to seek help and advice. Generalists have more spirit, more heart, because they have a wider frame of reference. Because of their expansive awareness, generalists are people of ability, talent, and enthusiasm who can bring their broad perspective to bear in specific fields of expertise. The doctor who is also a poet and philosopher is a superior doctor, one who can give so much more to his patients than just good medical skills.

Don't be afraid to stop one thing and start another. A talented, successful interior designer from Atlanta named Charles retired from his practice and is now lecturing, teaching, and painting botanicals, having shows every year. He has time to garden, travel, and enjoy a new chapter of his life.

Nothing is isolated. Let your expertise in one field fan your passions in all related areas. Some of your interests may not appear to be connected but, once you explore their depths, you discover that they are. My editor, who is also a writer, has edited several medical books as well as half a dozen books about the brain. Toni has decided to study human anatomy. Fascinated by the body's movement as a dancer, she is equally interested to learn more about pain. What causes pain? How can it be relieved? Early in the quiet of the morning while sipping coffee, she is studying anatomy, "I don't know where it will lead, but I'm excited I'm on this quest."

These expansions into new worlds help us by giving us new perspectives—we gain wisdom versus knowledge. We begin to see the interconnectedness of one thing to another in all aspects of our life, of ourselves and the universe. Think of the trunk of a tree as the generalist. This is the foundation for our entire life. The branches of the tree are specialists. The more support you have from the tree trunk, like the spine of your back, the more freedom you'll have as you move into new depths of study, research, and training.

The way I balanced the demands of learning and practicing my craft as a decorator was to spend all of my free time expanding my horizons. This was encouraged by my mentor, Mrs. Brown. So much of what I did when I was not at the office or with clients seemed to have fed my specialty.

As a young design student and decorator, I studied faux finishing, took a gilding course, and studied architecture. I went to museums, art galleries, concerts, the ballet, theater and movies. I started a personal library by browsing bookstores for remaindered books. I'd go to art and antique auction houses every week to scout and learn, and then go to the sales. The auction catalogues were an educational revelation to me early on.

Interior designing requires being able to envision something that does not exist. Certainly my trip around the world with my aunt amid my training at design school helped expose me to profound beauty as well as to great poverty and ugliness. It was during the month I spent in India in 1959 that I found new, vibrant, saturated colors and ideas for my career.

In addition to taking me around the world on her small salary as a pioneering social worker, my aunt also left me one thousand dollars in her will. This became the basis for an ongoing travel fund that has taken me to far-off places. Whenever I travel, I see more clearly how thrilling life's adventure is. On an island vacation I came up with a color scheme for a beach house on Fisher's Island in New York. The whole house was colored in a range of blues, with accents of pink to echo the sky, the water, sunrises and sunsets.

The more I studied, read, traveled, and gained experience about life, the more I was drawn to be a writer. Having a specialty allowed me to be considered an expert in one field—interior design. Society tends to reward specialists. I remember the day when I was told that I could no longer write the back page editorial for *McCall's* magazine, something I had loved doing for five years. The new owners wanted my column to be in the middle of the magazine, with me as the *decorating* expert. I had been writing a column entitled "Living Beautifully." Decorating is only a preparation for living. I quit. I'd worked hard to be able to write about living fully, not just about interior design.

There is a bigger picture that is huge. Keep expanding your curiosity. Don't be afraid. Once you make the daring plunge, there's no stopping you. Multiply your curiosity and fun; wear many different hats. Develop broad, general knowledge and experience. The universe is all yours to explore and enjoy.

EXPECT THE UNEXPECTED.

Motto of the Experiment for International Living

Open Presents Slowly

✳

THE OLDER I GET, THE MORE I SAVOR AND TREASURE
EVERY PRESENT I RECEIVE.

Eleanor McMillen Brown

A present is a love offering. Create a ritual, a celebration, a ceremony, when you open a gift. Wait until the appropriate time to relish the experience. You need to take time to laugh at a card that contains a joke, to feel the intimacy, the care and thoughtfulness that went into the gift.

Soak up the entire pleasure—the colorful ribbon, the bow, the wrapping paper, the box, the pastel tissue paper, and, ah, the gift. Whether you are alone or with friends or family, enhance the present moment. Light a candle. Play favorite music—I love to play Enya. Take time to fully appreciate, to relish, this generous, thoughtful gesture.

Over forty years ago when I went to work for Eleanor McMillen Brown's decorating firm, the doyenne of American interior design taught her young designers, "Order precedes beauty." We have to create an organized atmosphere around us in order to appreciate subtle beauty and grace. Years later when I wrote *Living a Beautiful Life*, this wise decorating principle proved to be useful. The book, about creating rituals, ceremonies, and celebrations, has a subtitle that is fitting: *500 Ways to Add Elegance, Order, Beauty, and Joy to Every Day of Your Life*. "Order precedes beauty" applies to larger life issues. Whenever we make a point of ritualizing life's present moments, we are applying this timeless truth.

I always open letters slowly, too. If I've just come back from a trip, I put them in a pile. I unpack, sort laundry; I wait until I'm relaxed and receptive to fully take in the words. Rushing through love letters from the heart diminishes their appreciation. This is indeed a special treat. Savor it as you would selecting a piece of chocolate from a box. Create meaning by slowing down the process.

PEOPLE CULTIVATE FIVE THOUSAND ROSES IN ONE GARDEN . . .
AND STILL THEY DO NOT FIND WHAT THEY SEEK . . .
AND YET WHAT THEY ARE SEEKING MAY BE FOUND
IN A SINGLE ROSE OR A DROP OF WATER.

Antoine de Saint-Exupery

Give Anonymously

❋

HOW FAR THAT LITTLE CANDLE THROWS HIS BEAMS!
SO SHINES A GOOD DEED IN A NAUGHTY WORLD.

Shakespeare

It is amazing how much can be accomplished when we don't insist on taking credit. Human nature inclines us to want to take credit for what we do and what we give. Why? What do we get from this? On a tangible level, we get the satisfaction of being recognized for our contribution. But we are endowed with a higher power that is nourished by a more elevated spirit. We are human and we are also divine. Giving anonymously is divine.

In the spirit of divine law, the more you give anonymously, the greater your sense of joy. When you see a need, helping without having your name attached can make you feel like the recipient of a great gift. The Chinese sage Lao Tsu taught us twenty-five hundred years ago, "Empty and be full." What you give away you receive instantly in the pleasure of goodwill.

People naturally have a tendency to do things that make them feel good. Giving anonymously makes you feel best. The mother of the late Episcopal bishop of New York Paul Moore was a woman of means and heart who quietly became the fairy godmother of Morristown, New

Jersey. Once she heard of a need, she found a silent way to provide funds immediately. A friend of mine in Texas anonymously provides free milk from her dairy farm to all poor families in her region.

When the foremost spokesman for the Unity movement, the late Eric Butterworth, learned there were no more funds to keep a local enterprise of the alternative medicine movement healthy, he quietly wrote a check sizeable enough to help this work stay alive. Approximately three in four people in America today use some form of alternative medicine.

A woman from Virginia who loves children and gardening gives the children in her church a hyacinth plant anonymously at Easter every year. In watching the children receive this fragrant, colorful potted plant from the minister as they leave the church, her joy is complete. Her own children promise to carry on this tradition when it is their turn.

There are very small ways of giving that cost us nothing in dollars and nearly nothing in time. When we don't litter, we are a part of a huge cumulative positive difference. Picking up litter when taking a walk is a habit that also adds to the larger good, giving us satisfaction. Leaving a picnic area clean for the next picnickers is a form of giving. Acting responsibly in a community, even when there are no rules, laws, or others present to require or enforce the behavior, is, in my view, an important form of giving. Who is it who said that character is what we do in the dark? Giving in all forms is a mirror into our essence. Whether you do a chore that needs doing, tidy up the office or kitchen, keep a bowl full of hard candy in the women's rest area, or bring flowers from your garden into the office to put on the tables in the cafeteria, you're giving of yourself and you are shining brightly in spirit.

When we sing with appreciation over the bounty of our lives, our hearts would burst if we didn't do our part and share our substance with others.

Be a giver. Give spontaneously. You don't give what you have, you give who you are. Be an angel. The more you give from a full heart, the less you need to be thanked. Buy an ice cream cone for the children behind you in line. Leave before the children can thank you. Giving enhances you. The more you give, particularly anonymously, the more you enrich your soul.

TO EXPERIENCE TRUE PERSONAL POWER REMEMBER THIS:
A RANDOM ACT OF KINDNESS SPREADS LIKE WILDFIRE BECAUSE
ALL OF US RESPOND TO LOVE. LOVE YOUR LIFE.

Blake Foster

Feel, Don't Just Think

✳

IT SEEMS TO ME WE CAN NEVER GIVE UP LONGING AND WISHING
WHILE WE ARE THOROUGHLY ALIVE. THERE ARE CERTAIN THINGS
WE FEEL TO BE BEAUTIFUL AND GOOD, AND WE MUST
HUNGER AFTER THEM.

George Eliot

When we feel strongly, we are better able to think the thoughts that produce good feelings. You are solely responsible for the way you feel. If your desire in life is well-being—happiness for yourself and others— feel first, then think. Enjoy any spontaneous outpouring of intensely good feelings.

Feelings arise through our senses and physical experiences and also through our thoughts. I'm acutely sensitive to my environment: to sights, sounds, colors, smells, and tastes, and to the textures of what I touch. What kinds of experiences make you feel intensely wonderful? What are you doing? What are you thinking? How are you feeling? I create my happiness out of intense positive feelings. I'm subjective and pay attention to my immediate emotions—not how I *should* feel, but how I actually feel. No one but you has complete access to your feelings. You know how you're feeling, second by second. By being aware of your true gut feelings, moment by moment, you will be living in the present moment.

You also will be more able to put yourself in an atmosphere that brings on more of these intensely wonderful feelings.

Do you want to feel better? The principle of the law of attraction holds that what we feel and think becomes our reality. This is as basic as the law of gravity. When you ask yourself, "How do I *feel* right *now*?" and the answer is, "wonderful," your feeling will influence your thinking, and thinking positive, life-enhancing thoughts will support your desire to feel well. If reason intrudes with intellectualizing or analysis, break the pattern. Ask yourself, "How do I feel?" Don't judge how you should feel, but literally, find out how you actually feel.

Try to be mindful of your physical sensations in each moment. Does your body have a sensation of lightness? Do you experience a sense of heightened interest or emotion? Do you feel a sense of wonder or awe? Sensations are generalized body feelings. There are philosophers who believe that sensation is the only source of true knowledge. There is an ethical doctrine that feeling is the only criteria of good. Do you believe that feeling leads you to truth?

Trust the role emotions play in your thinking. When you're in touch with your feelings, you understand that information is not inspiration. Reason without emotion is useless because it is not taking into account your happiness. Reason requires feeling to be complete; now you can empathize. It is good to have the capacity for logical, rational, and analytic thinking, but not at the expense of our emotional responses.

When we think, we ponder, we suppose, we consider, and we remember. But thinking doesn't always discern the bottom line as force-fully and accurately as your emotions do. We educate ourselves on issues and then tend to trust our emotions. I primarily form my opinions more from my feelings than from my intellect. My feelings empower me, inform me what I should do next, and guide me intuitively along my path.

Many brilliant people shun feeling intensely and claim to be "completely objective." But I believe you should let yourself be informed by your feelings and hunches. Beyond reason, there is some other faculty working in us that guides our understanding of what is true. Often my feelings are accompanied by a physical sensation. I feel a surge of energy. I get goose bumps. I have learned to trust these signs of insight and perception.

Our brain informs our mind: our mind controls our thoughts, mood and attitude. Do you believe that our emotions inform our minds? I believe a feeling wedded to thought is real power. Bringing our emotions and our intellect into partnership creates excellence that is both useful and wise. How do you feel in the presence of a great idea? The sensation is emotional, physical, spiritual, and intellectual. We have a surge of emotion, and have a rush of ideas in response.

When we are more mindful of feelings of joy or pain—our own and others'—we become more compassionate, more empathetic, more understanding. Our feelings guide us into self-love and love of others. When something feels right emotionally, it is probably right for you. The Buddhist tradition has essentially three meditative practices: (1) focused attention, (2) voluntarily cultivated compassion, and (3) open presence or pure awareness. Our thoughts, our emotions, and our sensations, fused in our feelings, are one.

BELIEVE THAT WITH YOUR FEELINGS AND YOUR WORK YOU ARE TAKING PART IN THE GREATEST; THE MORE STRONGLY YOU CULTIVATE THIS BELIEF, THE MORE WILL REALITY AND THE WORLD GO FORTH FROM IT.

Rainer Maria Rilke

Maintain Your Unique Friendships with Both Sexes

❋

FRIENDSHIP IS THE MARRIAGE OF THE SOUL.

Voltaire

When I was a young girl, I looked up to my father's father, a minister. Grandfather Johns was bigger than life to me. While I have always had meaningful friendships with both men and women, perhaps, without being conscious of it, I was seeking a male mentor. Looking back, I recognize that many of my male friends are older, accomplished professionals who have taught me so much.

Friendships with the opposite sex help men better understand their wives and mothers, just as these relationships help women know more about their fathers, sons, or brothers. Elderly friends provide us with a window on experience. They're often in a position to guide us along our path, providing opportunities and possibilities for our unfolding.

An older person may be better at seeing the bigger picture than someone with a more narrow focus who is busy juggling job and family. I find older people give good advice that is cautious and wise because they're uniquely positioned to encourage us in a positive way. Aristotle referred to these kinds of bonds as *friendships of character* as distinguished from *friendships of pleasure* or *friendships of utility*.

Because an older person doesn't usually want anything in return from you other than companionship, their advice may be less biased than advice received from a younger person or contemporary. Whether you need assistance in trying to decide whether to move to a new community or to buy a house, whether to take on a certain job or business transaction, where to go on vacation, or whether you should engage in or separate from a relationship—look to an older friend for helpful, thought-provoking ideas.

Making new connections with people who are different from us is a great gift we give ourselves. These less likely bonds broaden our view and take us out of our narrow worlds. The dear friends we have loved for years—as well as our spouse and children—enrich us but don't always stretch us. Our universe enlarges when we forge new and unique relationships. Be open and receptive to opportunities to get to know younger people, the elderly, small children, a nun, a healer, a waitress you meet at the diner, or a friendly bus driver.

Even in the most loving and nurturing families, none of us can detach from our specific roles—mother, father, child, sibling, or spouse. We all need to sometimes be free from that structure. Friends are our escape from the confines of function and position.

Be friendly to all so that you can connect with the variety of interesting people you meet every day, absorbing their insights, ideas, expertise, and unique take on life. The interchange is healthy and rewarding.

WITHOUT FRIENDS NO ONE WOULD CHOOSE TO LIVE,
THOUGH HE HAD ALL OTHER GOODS.

Aristotle

Unplug Technology with No Apologies

✻

IT'S AN ADDICTION . . . SOME PEOPLE CANNOT DEAL WITH DOWNTIME
OR QUIET MOMENTS. WITHOUT IT, WE ARE IN WITHDRAWAL.

John Ratey

I've made a deliberate decision to stay as unplugged as I can get away with, without giving up my freedom of choice. I want to be literally in touch with family, friends, clients, and acquaintances in order to live a full, content, happy life—not via e-mail or cell phone.

You are of another generation. I was formally educated before the advent of the personal computer. I read books, wrote papers with a fountain pen, sketched with a pencil, and painted with a brush and pigment.

I am in favor of all the time-saving devices technology offers us. But machines don't think or feel. We are not human machines; we are divine human beings. I enjoy working indoors with bright halogen lights. I also love to turn the lights out and go for a walk in the brilliant sunshine. No matter how necessary and useful, lamplight is a lower substitute for sunlight, just as scenic wallpaper is an imitation of a real view of nature.

Unplug regularly and get away. Too much time spent with technology causes fragmentation from humanity and separation from your intuitive nature. Because technology is so pervasive, like the odor of garlic, it permeates life, interfering with social interaction and communication. You begin to feel like a machine as you respond to all of your machines, losing sight of the subtle, significant qualities that connect you to your own purpose and meaning in life.

In extreme cases, technology can alienate someone from himself or herself, and others, causing the person to become withdrawn, unresponsive, and emotionally isolated. When technology becomes an addiction, the user becomes numb. When one becomes a slave to technology, there is no space for the soul to breathe and become nourished.

Machines break down. The model you have will soon be out-of-date. Then you will need the newer, better, and often more expensive brand. You believe it is necessary for survival and success. Technology begins to run you, rather than the other way around: when a phone is omnipresent, we believe we must always be in contact. But cellular phones have disrupted the commute on public transportation, where fights break out between those who are engaged in phone chat, sometimes aimlessly, and those who want quiet to read and think.

Technology doesn't sleep. It goes around the clock. Instantaneous communication has saved us time, but we are paying a price. We get sucked into thinking that we have to be connected constantly. We are not enjoying a mindful connection to our center, to our inner life. Our technological preoccupation has created disorientation, preventing the delicious immediacy of the present moment's clarity and purity—unless we can walk away and escape from our information overload.

There must be times when you rely purely on your five senses and your inner guidance. Reawaken yourself to the majestic beauty of the trees, sky, water, and flowers. Schedule time away from the hustle of the marketplace or the grating noise of the dishwasher, the washing machine, the clothes dryer, the hair dryer, the woof and drip of air-conditioning, and the inertia of the remote control.

I rented a cell phone the evening before Alexandra went into labor with her daughter Lily. The only other person who knew its number was Alexandra. The day after Lily's birth, I left the hospital in Washington, DC, to go have my hair done at four P.M. Bingo. The black-out of 2003. The first and only call to the rented cell phone that was ever attempted on was from Alexandra, who called from the hospital to tell me about the blackout. I had rented the phone in New York City. It didn't vibrate. It didn't ring. Once I was home, it was returned to the store with the cradle, the batteries, and the carrying case. I sighed with relief at again becoming officially "unplugged."

I remember when I left Mrs. Brown's firm to start Alexandra Stoddard, Incorporated, I deliberately chose to be low-tech. I designed some handsome stationery and wrote my estimates and invoices by hand. When I worked for the Singapore government just after I opened my firm, all the contracts were in my handwriting, written with a foun-tain pen. To this day, I write every draft of my books with a pen by deliberate choice. I find the fax machine enormously useful, but I pre-fer writing letters and postcards to using e-mail. I don't like the pres-sure of being in the position of having to immediately respond.

This low-tech choice works well for me. I recognize it would be dis-astrous for some people. When you're able to use technology to contain your exposure, increase efficiency, and not let it take over, you are in control, not the other way around.

We can use an answering machine so that we can return calls at our leisure. If you find a cell phone convenient so that you can choose when and where to call, try to think of it as a luxury, not a necessity. You can use the Internet to locate information quickly. But like everything else, such things can be overdone.

My conscious choice to remain low-tech in my business has not harmed me. I feel free from the continuous demands of others. At my own pace, when I can, I respond by telephone, fax, or letter. I prefer to keep the ink flowing in my pen and my heart beating to the rhythm of my soul.

We need to balance technology with nature: the sunrise and sunset, the moon, the stars, the tides, and the seasons. Take regular mini-vacations from everything that plugs in or requires batteries. Walking away is a form of meditation. You can be mindful of the blossoming almond tree, the beauty of having your family alone, together, for a picnic in the park far away from cell phones, beepers, and e-mail.

You'll never be able to keep up with everything without giving up life's true richness—time to reflect, to read, to wonder, to dream. When things get too busy-busy, too stressful, and you are nervous, anxious, and worried—walk away. You'll come back with a clearer perspective.

Give your soul some undivided attention. Unplug. Awaken your senses to new heights.

LIFE IS A SERIES OF MOMENTS.
EACH MOMENT SHOULD BE WELCOMED IN JOY AND RELINQUISHED IN JOY.

Deepak Chopra

Remember That Everyone Is Struggling

✳

RIGHT AND WRONG . . . WILL EVER CONTINUE TO STRUGGLE.

Abraham Lincoln

Our lower human nature tends to make us feel unique in our pain, in the stresses and strains of this earthly life. We ask, "Why me?"

Be kind and patient with yourself and others. Everyone is—in one way or another—fighting a hard battle. When we unite in a collective consciousness where we are all united but unique souls, we become more compassionate, more empathetic, more loving.

People, for the most part, are doing the best they can with their resources and circumstances. You are not defined by your troubles or your struggles. Continue to stay focused in the present moment where you have footing for a fresh start to build your future of well-being, balance, and inner peace. Try to keep your struggles to yourself. You have an inner guide you can consult. (I agree, though, that there are instances where people have serious mental, physical, and emotional problems that deserve professional counseling.) If you spend too much time talking about what's wrong, you focus on what is negative in your life. The more you think and talk about your problems, the more magnified they become. Focus your thinking on a cure, on a solution, on healing, on love. Turn your problems into challenging situations. Train your mind to see the big picture, keeping things in perspective. Life is too precious and fleeting to get bogged down in self-pity.

To be human is to experience pain and to overcome it. When you are struggling, be with loved ones who help you to smile and laugh through your tears. Remember what heals you. Is it going to a coffee house for an espresso and a fun outing? Is it going to a market and selecting some flowers to bring home and arrange? Is it going out in the sunlight for a long walk? A massage is always healing. Pain is to be overcome. You are bigger than this awful hurdle.

Know that others want to heal themselves also. What help can you provide? Even a little help is noted and appreciated. Everyone wants to live as good a life as possible in whatever situation they find themselves in.

Many people are often private about their pain, but by listening and being present, you can feel someone is hurting. Try not to be excessively sympathetic and focus too much on sadness. Instead, offer your love. Keep your energy positive. Be cheerful and be the bearer of good news, no matter how minor. Sometimes when someone is struggling, they want to keep a stiff upper lip. Through compassion, a big hug, a smile, you can remind them that they are supported and not alone.

Try to deal compassionately with people whose pain causes them to lash out in anger or bitterness. Listen, be still. Say you are sorry in order to soften your exit. A woman at her daughter's bridal dinner was in pain over the recent death of her husband. She lashed out at her daughter's fiancé. It was obvious to all of us who heard that she inwardly wished her husband were alive to be with her at the wedding.

We learn from our struggles, when all is temporarily not well. Always try to concentrate on what makes you feel good. You can help others to heal themselves by your blessing, wishing others well. Send out loving energy to the universe.

WE WILL NOW DISCUSS IN A LITTLE
MORE DETAIL THE STRUGGLE
FOR EXISTENCE.

Charles Darwin

When You Discover Something You Love, Stock Up

❄

When you discover a favorite author, buy as many of his or her books as you can afford for your own library. Buy several "for stock" to give as gifts to family and friends. When you find a blouse that you love, buy it in different colors. If you discover a favorite artist, start a collection. If you save and budget to buy one painting a year, think how beautiful your home will look and feel in twenty years. When a pianist's performance touches your soul, collect his or her CDs.

A friend has a mug collection from places that she and her husband visited, starting from their honeymoon in Maine. Peter began a collection of French and English eighteenth- and nineteenth-century brass carriage clocks thirty years ago and is still collecting. Another friend collects hats and displays them on a hat rack in his mudroom. Whenever I'm at his house and we go for a walk, I grab a hat off the rack. It makes the outing jauntier and I'm protected from the sun. I stock up on ribbons wherever I find them. I wrote in *Feeling at Home* and *Choosing Happiness,* one of my ten defining words is *ribbons.* My passion for ribbons has grown ever since childhood when I opened birthday presents. I find such beauty in my ribbons that I give them away as bookmarks or tied around gifts. I have a walk-in closet in our New York apartment that I call the ribbon chest. Reward: comfort and inspiration every day.

I stock up on bud vases and flower containers because I love to arrange flowers. I have a weakness for pastel ballet slippers and stock up when I find new colors. I stock up on fountain pens, ink cartridges, and French writing pads to keep me inspired. When I sometimes go to Unity services on Sunday mornings at Avery Fisher Hall at Lincoln Center, I stock up on Eric Butterworth's inspirational tapes on metaphysics; I listen to them when I'm ironing, meditating, or traveling.

Stock up on experiences, not just things. Open up to living more fully. When you discover that you really like to stay home on Tuesday nights to read, do more of it. Make it a ritual. If you discover that you enjoy going to Sunday brunch at a neighborhood restaurant, plan to do it regularly. If you discover that you love going to Vermont in October to see the foliage and stay in a favorite inn, stock up and go every year. Life is short. If you love music, buy a series of tickets for your local symphony. If you love art, sign up for a lecture series at your favorite museum. In the summer on Saturday mornings, we go to the largest farmers' market in Connecticut in Stonington Village. We enjoy visiting with the farmers as we select organic tomatoes, melons, peaches, and berries, as well as zinnias and sunflowers. We look forward to this stocking up all week. If you enjoyed your evening at a Broadway musical, stock up and go to another one that has rave reviews. Treat yourself to these memorable celebrations regularly.

Do the things you most enjoy. Do them often. Stock up. When you discover something you love, do more in love.

CAN ONE DESIRE TOO MUCH OF A GOOD THING?

Shakespeare

Don't Be on Time, Be Early

❋

YOU MAY DELAY, BUT TIME WILL NOT.

Benjamin Franklin

When you plan a meeting with another person or a group, out of respect for yourself and others, be early. Plan to be there fifteen minutes ahead of time. It is better to leave plenty of time for contingencies. Don't leave anything to chance. You could run into all sorts of problems—a last-minute phone call, car trouble, an accident, or construction on the highway.

When you're late, you're harried. The first thing that people who are late do is to breathlessly regale others with all the problems they had getting there. It's hard for humans to have the foresight to allow enough time to be on time. We tend to underestimate how long it takes to get somewhere. When you can, do a trial run. This is not always necessary, but it can be extremely helpful. Timing how long it will take you to get somewhere—to find a parking place, the right elevator bank, or the right room—can keep you from being nervous and stressed over things you can easily control.

There's a wonderful woman who is a literary escort who drives authors to book signings and radio and television interviews. Sally is my favorite because she does a dry run: she knows the side entrance into the studio parking lot; she knows where to go and how to get there and back, making me relaxed so I can enjoy myself and do my best. Conversations with Sally along the way are enlightening, too. She is relaxed because she is prepared.

You set things up to work to your benefit when you show up early. Discipline yourself to be early so that you can be in top form, enjoying the success of having thought ahead, allowing ample time. We can't take a chance of making a tight connection in an unfamiliar airport with the ever-present risk of security delays. Be early for each event by being realistic about how long it will take you to get from where you are to where you're meant to be.

Once there, you can freshen up, read, or go for a walk. The only exception is a dinner party: it's rude to arrive early. (I'd be the hostess in the bathtub. I always take a bath at the last moment so I won't get sweaty in my party clothes doing last-minute preparations.) But for all professional appointments, cultivate the habit of showing up early.

As a trial lawyer, Peter arrives at the courthouse early. He can chat with the court reporter and clerk and adjust his files. If documents are missing, he has time to ask his assistant to get him the papers. He has time to locate the courtroom if it has been reassigned. The client is guided to the right place at the right time with extra minutes to orient and gain a sense of confidence and order. The stage is set and all is well. So far!

Before I give a lecture, I always arrive at the designated place at least one hour ahead of time. I get settled in. I feel the energy of the space, try the microphone, test the equipment and lighting. I can fix my hair and makeup, and be poised, centered, and relaxed. There is time to get a new battery for the slide projector, if necessary. If I've been invited to go on a television show, I go to the city the night before so that I can relax, knowing that I don't have to worry about a plane being delayed—or worse, canceled due to weather. These are not minor matters in any sense; experience teaches us that indifference to punctuality can be trou-blesome if not disastrous. Promptness is a virtue.

People who are habitually late are not in control of their lives. I find it rude because they are thinking (if at all) about themselves, and not oth-ers. All the great people I know and admire who have made significant contributions to society understand this key to civility and success of allowing plenty of time, by starting early, to assure that they will arrive promptly.

Being early celebrates and honors an event. Everything in life has aspects of give and take. Every action has an effect. If clients keep me waiting, they're putting me off my schedule, wasting my time. Don't keep doctors waiting; it throws off their rhythm all day and is a discourtesy to the doctor and fellow patients. No one is entitled to think that his or her time is more valuable than someone else's. No one is inferior or supe-rior to anyone else.

Make a special effort to be early when you meet an elderly person because it honors them. Sometimes you are the highlight of their day. You can reciprocate the sense of importance they attach to the meeting. Older people tend to be early. When picking up a child, be there wait-ing. This helps children to feel the total security of your love. They know they can count on you.

Dignify your sense of connectedness with others by giving every event ample time and space. Be enthusiastic, be reliable, be early.

I ALWAYS LEAVE FOR THE AIRPORT AN EXTRA HOUR EARLY,
SO I CAN PRACTICE WALKING MEDITATION THERE.
FRIENDS WANT TO KEEP ME UNTIL THE LAST MINUTE,
BUT I RESIST. I TELL THEM THAT I NEED THE TIME.

Thich Nhat Hanh

Listen to the Wisdom of Your Children

❋

FEEL THE DIGNITY OF A CHILD. DO NOT FEEL
SUPERIOR TO HIM, FOR YOU ARE NOT.

Robert Henri

To a child, the world is miraculous. Look up to your children as your true teachers. They are open, receptive, spontaneous, and intuitive. Children are intimately connected to their physical and emotional selves. They teach us what it is like to be completely in touch with our feelings, to be in many ways more authentic.

Children know, naturally, their own needs and wants. If they are thirsty, they drink. If they are hungry, they eat. If they are tired, they sleep. If they feel frisky, they run around, expending some of their excess energy. If a child doesn't have a toy, he'll make believe, making "pancakes" in the sandbox or serving tea in an empty cup. They're resourceful, having profound imaginative powers that most adults cannot comprehend. They make up and make believe.

You can never give too much love to a child. They deserve it regardless of circumstances. The more pure positive energy you communicate to children, the better they thrive. Our responsibility is to create an environment to encourage them to unfold.

Ask your child deep, meaningful questions. Know that your children are old, wise souls. You will only be with them a short time. Show up for their events; you are their chief cheerleader. When I went early to one of Brooke's basketball games, I went out on the gym floor, dribbled the basketball, and from behind my head with two hands, I threw the ball into the basket. Whoosh! Her coach saw this and everyone clapped. I scored with her and her team, big-time. This rare hit took me back to fun years playing basketball on a school team.

Pay attention to your children's wild requests. Ask your child what she wants to do; within reason, do it. Once when I asked Brooke where she wanted to go on a mother-daughter groove during her February winter break from school, she responded, "Paris." We ditched Peter for a week and the Stoddard girls, using frequent-flyer mileage, were off to Paris. Be prepared for many surprises, many detours, and many adventures.

Every child is full of wisdom. When Alexandra was a teenager, we were alone in the kitchen one day and she told me, with a giggle, "You know, Mom, we wouldn't spend time with you if you weren't fun to be with." I laughed and realized how honest and wise she was. Be there, listen, and enjoy your children's vibrant, pure love of life. Become the person they will choose to be with and believe in their greatness.

OUR CHILDREN ESSENTIALLY NEED TWO THINGS FROM US:
(1) THEY NEED TO BE RECOGNIZED FOR WHO THEY REALLY ARE.
(2) THEY NEED US TO CREATE AN EXAMPLE FOR THEM OF
HOW TO LIVE EFFECTIVELY IN THE WORLD OF FORM.

Shakti Gawain

Tell Yourself
You Have Done
Nothing Wrong

✻

HIS BEST COMPANIONS,
INNOCENCE AND HEALTH.

Oliver Goldsmith

There are going to be people in life who act badly. No matter how kind, helpful, or productive you are, people involved in your life might suddenly hurt you.

Sometimes, but clearly not always, there are two sides to a story. It's hard to admit when we are wrong. If someone accuses you of inappropriate behavior, try to see the situation from both sides. Examine your behavior. Were you selfish? Rude? Irresponsible? Ask yourself, "Should I go back and revisit what really happened?" Were you feathering your own nest at someone else's expense? Try to see the situation from their point of view.

While you are analyzing the facts of what really happened, be calm. Don't let it consume you. Take whatever time it takes to come to a conclusion. If you were wrong, see what you can do to make amends. Being truly sorry for whatever you did, and showing remorse, frees you from living with a crippling guilty conscience.

If you haven't done anything wrong, you can tell the one who accuses you that you have done nothing wrong. Say it in a soft, sincere voice. Make good eye contact. You are now free to move on.

PEOPLE ARE LIKE STAINED-GLASS WINDOWS. THEY SPARKLE AND SHINE WHEN THE SUN IS OUT, BUT WHEN THE DARKNESS SETS IN, THEIR TRUE BEAUTY IS REVEALED ONLY IF THERE IS A LIGHT FROM WITHIN.

Elisabeth Kübler-Ross, M.D.

Learn to Style Your Own Hair

✳

HAPPINESS BELONGS TO THOSE WHO ARE
SUFFICIENT UNTO THEMSELVES.

Arthur Schopenhauer

Don't look at my hair, look at your own. I'm not the best example of my advice, but the principle is important to understand. My hair is gray and curly; in humidity it is kinky. I often look as though I have a mop on my head.

However, I don't despair. I have flat ears and I look and feel somewhat handsome with my hair smoothed with some styling gel and pulled back in a clip. But that's me, not you. You must be self-sufficient. If you have a demanding hairdo, you are setting yourself up for time, expense, and a schedule that depends on visits to professionals. In bad weather, humidity, on vacations, or on business trips, you're setting yourself up for some failure: Deep frustration!

There are times when I love to escape by myself to have my hair done. Just because you can style your own hair doesn't mean you should. But I'm always conscious of the expense, the time it takes to get to the salon, the waiting around. When I try to read, the stylist wants to chitchat. Having your hair professionally *cut well* is essential so that you can style it yourself on a regular basis. A good haircut is always worth

the time, effort, and expense to accomplish the look you want. But paying for someone to wash and dry your hair might be considered a treat
rather than a routine necessity.

You need the freedom to move through your life unrestricted by the
details of your hair. You can't find a hair salon in every town, and many
are closed on Sundays, Mondays, and holidays. If you master your own
hairstyle, you won't get caught with your hair looking horrible at inconvenient times and places where you can't get it done. You can go to the
gym more often, knowing you can easily wash and style your hair and
go straight to work.

Of course there are times when you will want to be pampered. But
value your time, freedom, and spontaneity—learn to do your own hair.

There are other "nice, but not necessary" things we do that are time-
consuming, expensive, and may feel good, but may make our life less efficient, less self-sufficient, and more labor-intensive in the long run.
Manicures, pedicures, waxing, and facials should be feel-good treats, not
necessities that too often become costly drags on our time and our sense
of freedom and autonomy. We start to think that we must have them in
order to look good and feel good.

After having a rare facial several years ago, the owner of the salon
insulted me when I went to pay the bill, telling me I had dry skin in
an attempt to sell me hundreds of dollars worth of lotions and
potions. She tried earnestly to convince me that I needed these expensive products.

Learn to style your own hair is a metaphor: Do what makes life work
well for you and weed out those things that add unnecessary time,
expense, and headaches. Living simply wherever you can and not buying (literally and figuratively) into cultural pressures to act and look a
particular way makes us feel free. Advertising is designed to make us
feel inadequate. Focus on your inner beauty that shines through makeup,

face-lifts, or hair coloring. When you're happy with who you are, your smile will make you look good and others feel good.

LIFE IS A SUCCESSION OF LESSONS WHICH MUST BE LIVED
TO BE UNDERSTOOD.

Emerson

Don't Assume Anything

❋

LIFE HAS NOT TAUGHT ME TO EXPECT NOTHING,
BUT SHE HAS TAUGHT ME NOT TO EXPECT SUCCESS TO BE THE
INEVITABLE RESULT OF MY ENDEAVORS.

Alan Paton

Assuming things is a sign of laziness, being casual, not checking to ensure that things work out well, can cause inordinate unhappiness. Check, check, check. Have you ever taken a new friend to a restaurant that turned out to be closed for renovations? Don't assume you can find a place to stay when you arrive in a strange town. How do you know for certain that the ice on the lake is strong enough to skate on?

Assuming you have the answers can be self-defeating. Ask carefully the necessary questions. Be a free spirit, but be diligent so you can enjoy your freedom without avoidable mishaps. Seek and find out what is true and accurate. We all make mild assumptions every day. We assume there is enough oil and gas in the car, a container of milk in the refrigerator, an extra cartridge for the fax machine, or enough AA batteries for the Walkman. We assume that everyone has been notified about the conference call. We assume that all participants have been sent the agenda for the meeting. We assume our spouse has the tickets, the cash, and the passports. Ask. Check. Have a list so you'll remember to bring whatever you need to wherever you are going. I make these suggestions because I have violated all of them over the years. Mea culpa.

Years ago, an assistant told me that she had scheduled me to give a slide presentation on color in California. When I arrived, I learned that the subject of my talk was not color but *Living Beautifully Together*. It was pretty goofy trying to apply my visuals to "relationships." I did the best I could, but it was not—to say the least—my best. Now, I always talk directly to the client group I am working with to be sure that I have the facts. The assistant "assumed," she told me, that the group would want my newest book title on color for my talk, but that wasn't accurate.

Human beings, in trying to accomplish something, should not assume that things have been done in advance. Assume that something hasn't been done until you know it has been completed to your satisfaction. When we delegate work to others, we should still spot-check, because we are personally responsible. We shouldn't pass the blame on to others. Especially when things are outside your responsibility, avoid disasters by reconfirming dates, times, places. Be sure you have enough cash for contingencies. Think through the consequences, and plan accordingly. It's true: success is yours; failure is an orphan.

People forget to do things they promised to do. They stand us up. They change an agenda without asking us or even informing us. Reconfirm appointments, lunch and dinner dates. My godmother was so upset after her son died that she told me the funeral was on Saturday at eleven A.M. We flew to Boston and went to the church to learn that the service was actually a memorial . . . the following Saturday. Another time we hosted a special Tuesday luncheon to celebrate the *first* day of spring only to discover that March 21 was on Wednesday, not Tuesday. We, as well as the printer, hadn't rechecked the calendar. One year, my parents forgot to put my name on the family Christmas card. They listed my brothers, my sister . . . and the dog.

Making a habit of assuming leads to carelessness and a lack of effec-tiveness. Instead, anticipate and focus. The more you care, the less you'll take for granted.

DON'T ASSUME A DAMN THING.

J. Edward Lumbard

Have Your Own Mad Money

❋

LOVE, AND DO WHAT YOU LIKE.

Saint Augustine

You need your own money that is not committed to family needs. For your dignity, pleasure, and independence, this is terribly important. Keep your mad money separate from household funds. It is not shameful to have financial independence; it is essential. Don't find yourself beholden to anyone. A woman should never have to ask for money from her spouse to do what she feels is right at any particular time. Keep a certain amount of mystery.

I don't believe it is appropriate to spend your spouse's money as mad money. That isn't what mad money is. Mad money is yours. You have to have some of your own money to spend without restrictions. This can be a touchy issue among couples.

Where does this mad money come from? Mad money is accumulated from many unexpected places: a small inheritance from a grandmother or aunt, a freelance job assignment, a fee from consulting work you've done—or a cash gift from a parent or spouse. Dividends and income from your investments—no matter how small—can add up. If you sell inherited antiques or a valuable object that was given to you, the money you receive should become yours to conserve and yours alone to spend.

Even on a tight budget, you can enjoy going to a café for your favorite coffee drink or you can buy flowers or books or a gift for a friend. You need to have the financial freedom to go on a retreat or lake vacation or to buy new clothes after you've lost weight. How can you enjoy giving your spouse birthday presents or a surprise weekend away if you don't have some money of your own? When you treat your spouse to dinner on the town after a show, you pay. Where does this money come from? Your mad money.

Having your own mad money gives you lots of opportunities for some cheap thrills. You can buy some pretty cocktail napkins that catch your eye or buy a handwoven basket at a craft fair. It's fun to browse in a thrift shop for costume jewelry or to buy a brightly colored scarf from a street vendor.

Dip into this mad money to your heart's content without having to ask permission. You are in charge—have your independent means. For those of you who *have* indulged, you know the pleasure and freedom's joy.

CERTAINLY THERE ARE LOTS OF THINGS IN LIFE THAT MONEY WON'T BUY, BUT IT'S VERY FUNNY—HAVE YOU EVER TRIED TO BUY THEM WITHOUT MONEY?

Ogden Nash

Move Your Feet

※

NOTHING IS MORE REVEALING THAN MOVEMENT. ACTIONS DO SPEAK.

Martha Graham

Make tracks—footprints in the sand. Jump in the ocean of life. Do it now. Get going. There are so many miraculous opportunities waiting for you.

Move your feet in the direction that is most favorable for your living up to your full potential. Doing is essential to accomplishing the goal of ultimate happiness. When you choose to move your feet, your energy and enthusiasm will increase. Act on your impulses. Be spontaneous. When you have a good idea, jump up and do something about it. When you are inspired, act immediately. If not now, when? Don't procrastinate. Easy things become hard, and hard things become impossible, when you put them off. Aristotle taught us twenty-five hundred years ago that once we know, once we have an impulse, we should act: he rightly called this "active virtue."

You are full of desires, wishes, things you want to experience and manifest. We can't just sit around asking questions. The answers, in most cases, are in our action; in the moving of our energy. When you have fire in your belly and you move in the direction of your goals and dreams, there will be nothing sluggish or lazy about you. The Chinese have a saying that the worm doesn't go to the hinge. Keep moving. Being passive is frustrating and depressing to your life force, your source energy. You want to wear out, not rust out.

Seize the opportunity at hand. We are our actions. Let them speak for you; they are persuasive. Actions do speak louder than words. You have to reach out to get what you desire. Bet on yourself. No one but you can literally move you.

We live our life in chapters. Each phase, from childhood to old age, can be rich with experiences, activities, and growth. What stage are you in now? What will your life be like in five years? What do you want to accomplish that you haven't begun? What steps are you taking toward your goals? What, for heaven's sake, is keeping you from moving your feet?

How do you get into action? How do you get past the little voice inside you—or the louder ones outside—that say, *"You can't"*? Eliminate the word *can't*. Shorten it to *can*. Recall the children's book *The Little Engine That Could,* "I think I can, I think I can, I think I can . . . I thought I could, I thought I could, I thought I could."

Don't take no for an answer. Don't let anyone frustrate you, discourage you, or tell you what you can't do. I've made it a point to never ask someone to do something for me that was not possible. I once had an assistant who told me, "I *can't* do *that,*" one too many times. I suggested she go work for a firm where she could tell her boss, "I can do that."

Push yourself through the barriers of fatigue and self-doubt. Go beyond what you've been able to accomplish before. Stretch yourself until you get in the zone, until you're in the swing, in the flow, in the groove. Until you give yourself all you have, you will be wasting your pure potential.

What do you want to do? Who or what is keeping you from fulfilling your goal? It really doesn't matter how long it takes to bring something forth, as long as you move your feet and begin.

I am friends with a fifty-year-old woman who has two teenage daughters. Erica is happily married and has her own business creating licensing products for celebrities. She is also an artist. Her dream was to have a one-person show, be surrounded by family and friends, and cheer everyone with a champagne toast surrounded by her own paintings. When she did, she sold out the show, had another successful one a year later, and she is now at New York University doing graduate work studying filmmaking. Erica swims, plays tennis well, and is an accomplished photographer. She skis, sails, cooks, and loves to have friends over; she's well read, she's funny, and she's one of the happiest people I have ever known.

Erica knows how to have fun. One of the secrets to her energetic enthusiasm is her sense of spontaneity. If our rosebushes are looking particularly gorgeous, she'll fly out of her house with her camera and use three rolls of film taking photographs of them, then do a chalk drawing and enter it in a garden show. She catches her fun on the wing. A dozen organic eggs bought Saturday morning at the farmers' market are an excuse to have some neighbors over for omelets for supper on the deck to watch the sunset. Joyful spontaneity—moving her feet—is her secret.

When we first move ourselves, then the universe seems to tune in to what we want to achieve. Follow your heart. What is your next step? Take it. Live it. Do it. Get moving.

SHUN IDLENESS.
IT IS A RUST THAT ATTACHES ITSELF TO THE MOST BRILLIANT METALS.

Voltaire

Overlook Things

❋

Many well-meaning people feel it is their duty to complete every task right away. Everything in the house or apartment must be meticulous all the time. All the deadlines at work must be met, often at the expense of our life at home. But will we be happier if we finally get all the recent photographs of the children into that album we keep talking about? Will we really be happier if we stay until dawn at the office to finish a report and get caught up on our paperwork? We have all known that nagging sense of urgent duty, of constant chores to be crossed off the "to do" list.

While I'm a great believer that order precedes beauty, we nonetheless have to strike a balance by putting some things off. We cannot finish every task or get it all done. Be able to sincerely say to yourself that you can and *will* overlook things. Everyone else regularly drops the ball—you can do it sometimes, too. It's not naughty. Don't create impossibly high standards for yourself. Living is a messy business. There will be piles of newspapers to throw out, sheets to change, your spouse's muddy sneakers by the back door, junk in the back of the car, and stuff at the bottom of your in-box. You'll be in harmony when you let some things go. What will you let go?

Of course, for each of us there are certain things we won't overlook. I find a well-made bed can bring an immediate sense of calm and order to my life. I like my clothes to be neat in my closet. Having the towels folded in the bathroom and the countertop clear and uncluttered is soothing. I like a clear space on my office desk to greet me in the morning.

When we clear off the front hall table of mail, newspapers and magazines before dinner, we feel well ordered. The flowers are more visible and appreciated without all the papers around. But why not put off going to the post office today when you can spend the time instead finding a present for the wedding you will soon attend? Why not plan in advance what you will wear to look your best and not be frazzled when the day arrives?

Find ways to strike a happy balance between what you do and what you choose not to do. You can't cook your dinner if the kitchen is a wreck from the children's meal, but for now you can overlook the mess on your desk because you don't have enough time to attack it and also do the dishes before you start to cook dinner. (Sometimes when my desk looks frighteningly messy, I put a small tablecloth over it to soothe my mind until I get back to work.) When you don't have small children to attend to, you may like to come home to a sink cleared of dirty dishes, ready for your dinnertime meal preparation. But when you have toddlers, you have to choose to deal with the kitchen mess over the desk disaster. Overlook the stains on your living room chairs if you can't get them out and you can't afford to recover them. Overlook the mud on the children's clothes when they come back from the park until you have time in the laundry room to apply your spot cleaner and Clorox 2.

We also have to overlook certain things in our relationships in order to enjoy our daily life at home, as well as at work. If you have to pick up after your spouse, but he's wonderful with the children, you may overlook his behavior. At work, you don't have to rise to the bait with an insulting coworker. Take things at ease. No situation is perfect. If there were perfection, we'd have no way of further improving our lives. The challenge for us is to be able to continue to strive for excellence. If we constantly strive for perfection, experience shows that we run the risk of alienating all our relationships and suffering burnout and depression—or worse.

You owe it to yourself to take care of your health, possessions, and your home, while maintaining a sense of balance, proportion, and humor despite the current fashion of extreme perfectionism, the militant way of putting off daily enjoyment and fun.

THE ART OF BEING WISE IS THE ART OF KNOWING WHAT TO OVERLOOK.

William James

Preparation Is Paramount

❋

THE MOST IMPORTANT THING ABOUT GETTING SOMEWHERE
IS STARTING RIGHT WHERE WE ARE.

Bruce Barton

Careful preparation shows our good intentions. When we don't take preparation seriously and "wing it," we often wind up regretting it. In most areas of our life, the more we put into something, the more we get out of it. Being prepared is a courtesy to others and a blessing to ourselves. The more I prepare for an event, the more pleasure I feel in the process, the greater my feeling of satisfaction with the results. When I'm prepared, I have confidence, because I'm able to be myself and be enthusiastic about the work.

There is no substitute for this behind-the-scenes hard work. Do your homework, your research. When we are well prepared, things tend to move forward harmoniously and turn out well. If mishaps occur, you'll have the mental clarity to handle them and do your best.

Preparation begins with identifying what you want to accomplish, anticipating what your needs will be, and preparing a backup plan by asking yourself "what if?" What if the technician doesn't show up for a slide presentation? What if it rains on the day of the wedding ceremony that you'd planned to hold in the garden? What if a client doesn't like scheme A? What if you're asked at the last minute to be the guest speaker at a dinner meeting because the intended speaker got sick? What if you learn that a severe hurricane is headed toward your house?

Take each commitment you say yes to seriously, and give it your all. Start your preparations as early as possible. Whether you are preparing for an examination, a legal trial, an interview, or a lecture, or organizing a meeting, arranging a retreat, having a baby, or planning a wedding, the better your front work, the more confident you'll be and the more rewarding the experience.

If you are having a dinner party, rather than combining new recipes in an unfamiliar menu, do a trial run beforehand. Experiment on your family to see how it all tastes and looks. Determine the timing details ahead of the event. Encourage your spouse or companion to help out with drinks and desserts. Your confidence will make you freer to be a gracious hostess.

If you need to confront someone about something important, whether on the telephone or in person, write down important words and phrases and practice aloud. Preparing will help you find the most effective way of expressing your concerns. Think and feel what the person's reaction might be. By anticipating the other person's response, we can be more open, more rational, and more focused during the interaction.

Before going to the doctor's office, write down your questions. Don't assume that you'll remember everything. You will have only a few minutes of this busy professional's undivided attention.

When preparing to step into a new role, job, or level of responsibility, you are starting from scratch. You can't coast or skim the surface, relying on your past success. I know of a Harvard professor who throws his notes away after he teaches a course so that he will stretch himself to study and grow, bringing fresh research and insights to his new students. I now prepare each talk I give for the particular audience I will address, tailoring my remarks to their individual requests or expectations.

When I was invited to speak at the Omega Institute at a four-day Heart of Happiness conference, I was happy to be teaching. I took this invitation seriously. I immediately designated a spiral notebook for preparatory notes and research. I made an outline of what I wanted to cover in the three hours in the classroom. I studied several hours daily for almost a year. I read and reread books by other speakers who were also speaking at the event. Preparation made all the difference: I was able to talk about *Choosing Happiness* with conviction and confidence.

When I take on a new decorating client, I see what's available in textiles, rugs, furniture, objects, and art. I gather ideas and samples before I have my first working session with the client. Knowing what's available is the first step in preparation. After carefully learning what the client envisions, I show them scheme A, scheme B, and scheme C. By checking stock before I show a fabric or rug sample, I may save months on the installation date.

Whether you're an architect, a designer, a lawyer, a writer, a teacher, a student, an actor, a dancer, an artist, or a concert pianist, be original in each new project. Show your evolution, how you've expanded beyond what you'd accomplished yesterday.

We need to be inwardly prepared as well as outwardly organized for excellence. We need enough sleep, to eat properly, and to be calm and centered. Take time to be at your best by always being prepared for what you want in life. Do your homework. Be realistic. Be the best that's in you.

Preparation, never forget, is paramount.

TO COMPREHEND IS TO KNOW A THING AS WELL AS
THAT THING CAN BE KNOWN.

John Donne

The Five-Hour Rule

❋

THE PERSONAL LIFE OF EVERY INDIVIDUAL IS BASED ON SECRECY,
AND PERHAPS IT IS PARTLY FOR THAT REASON THAT CIVILIZED MAN IS SO
NERVOUSLY ANXIOUS THAT PERSONAL PRIVACY SHOULD BE RESPECTED.

Anton Chekhov

I have written numerous decorating books, but have never written
about guest rooms. I'd lose my peace of mind if I had unwanted guests
staying with us. Consequently, I developed the five-hour rule: I choose
never to be with anyone for longer than five hours at a stretch. By that
time I'm talked out. I've listened enough. I need time away. I need to
replenish my inner well. I need to be free to use my energy in whatever
ways feel right at the time. If a visit can't be complete within five con-
secutive hours, I say no more without a substantial break. We can't be
made captive without our permission. I spend time with people on my
terms in order to be true to myself.

Having houseguests violates the five-hour rule. This is especially
true with in-laws. I can't imagine any situation more awkward than having in-laws come and stay with you. It is always a trap—everyone is
together under one roof for days while you and your spouse whisper
and fight in the bathroom. While they loaf around, you feel awkward
doing anything—paying bills, making phone calls, or doing laundry—

with someone always there, sitting silently or trying to make conversation with you.

Having houseguests often sows bad feelings that people are too embarrassed to bring up. The conscientious host wants everything to be "perfect" for the guests, wishing that their every need be met. House repairs and yard work are done, windows are cleaned, flowers arranged, sheets ironed, the table set, and a fire laid. All of this benefits home and hearth, but it is a lot of pressure.

Even the most companionable of visits may make the hosts feel stretched between work, home chores, entertaining, and feeling that they must keep their guests occupied. Not to mention the financial strains that can occur from the cost of extra food in the refrigerator for breakfast, having the pantry stocked, extra soft drinks, wines, and liqueur, fancier and more elaborate meals, dining out, and going to the movies or a concert or lecture.

Considerate guests may also feel awkward, relaxing in a place not their own, unable to have total privacy for *their* discussions. When there are children at home, they are forced to make their bedrooms immaculate, be charming to the company, dress attractively, pass hors d'oeuvres, and perhaps be subject to endless picture-taking sessions. Everyone needs breaks. The five-hour rule is the answer.

How do we tactfully set limits, or break an existing pattern where the family has been coming to stay for long holidays for years? One nearly desperate daughter-in-law moved to a smaller house to eliminate the guest room. When the mother-in-law offered to pay for a sofa bed for the children's playroom, she bought two large pet rabbits and had a huge cage built for the playroom. Apparently, it cut the visits down considerably.

There are less radical solutions: maybe you can offer to visit your in-laws, staying in a nearby hotel, motel, inn, or bed-and-breakfast. If your in-laws' feelings are hurt because you aren't staying with them, explain that the children are rambunctious and you feel your spouse's family will be more comfortable having some free time and not having to take care of your family every minute. You can be upbeat and let them know how excited you are to see them, while still adhering to the five-hour rule.

When I was newly married and terribly insecure, my former mother-in-law came to spend three nights in our tiny apartment. She had to sleep on a pullout sofa in the living room. It was so dreadful having her so close, sharing the only bathroom, overhearing our whispers, giving us endless advice we were not seeking. I cried myself to sleep. After she reluctantly left, I tipped the building superintendent five dollars (a generous sum in 1961) to remove the sofa bed (our only sofa!) from the apartment living room.

You need your privacy. No home is big enough, with thick enough walls, to have another familiar tribe so close. When visiting friends and family, stay at a hotel. They can see you before, during, and after meals—for five hours—but then everyone gets a chance to nap, read, be intimate, bathe, and refresh in between the catching up.

You have every right to set your own standards and maintain your own customs. How many hours feels right to you? Set the record straight.

WE ALL FIND TIME TO DO WHAT WE REALLY WANT TO DO.

William Feather

Express an Original Point of View

✻

IF YOU DO NOT EXPRESS YOUR OWN ORIGINAL IDEAS,
IF YOU DO NOT LISTEN TO YOUR OWN BEING,
YOU WILL HAVE BETRAYED YOURSELF.

Rollo May

You are unique. The universe wants to hear from you. Find a way to awaken us to your vision.

There is so much inside you that is completely original and fresh—pure you. Believe you have new wisdom to share, and put it out there. Others make their voices heard; now it is your turn. Take what you believe is true from the past and add your own understanding and interpretation. You have the distinct advantage of having access to all the efforts of great minds and souls who came before you. This is a rich inheritance but not, I hope, the final vision. Go further. Be an innovator. Don't worship the giants who came before you; let their inspiration help enlarge your consciousness, guide you on *your own* path. Stand on their shoulders for your new vision. Each of us is challenged to go beyond what has ever been thought. Dare to think and share thoughts that have never been expressed before.

Once your understanding has been expanded, it can never go back, contentedly, to where it was. You see through things, without bias, fears, or compromise, getting right to the heart of the truth. Try not to let other people divert or discourage you from your quest to add your originality to the world. If you don't make your contributions, you will never know why you are here or how you should live your life. By expressing yourself, by being honest to your core, you are making a significant contribution to yourself and to the world.

There is no one else like you in the world. You, through your original point of view, are helping to shape, mold, and transform the consciousness of future generations. If there is something you've discovered that you feel is significant, express it now.

I AM NO PHILOSOPHER, BUT IF CONTINUITY IS ANYTHING, IT IS IN THIS. BRIGHT PICTURES IN THE DARK OF THE MIND, EACH AN ECHO OF SOMETHING, BUT STILL UNIQUE.

Claude Monet

Don't Save the Best for the Last

❋

I GIVE YOU THE CONTAGIOUS INFLUENCE OF JOY, WITH WHICH YOU MAY
INFECT ALL PERSONS WITH A NEW DIMENSION OF ABUNDANT LIVING.

Eric Butterworth

Let your joy in life be unrestrained. Take a vacation this year while everyone is healthy. Too busy to go? You'll be busy next year, too, so if not now, when? Here, now, are the best of times. Don't put off fun. Don't put yourself last. What pleasure we have now affects what comes later. You'll never be caught up; you'll never get all your work done, so start living joyfully now. It is later than you think. Don't save the best for last—last is often, sadly, too late. Live each day as though it were the first as well as the last.

You are at the banquet. Don't hold back. Do what you really want to do now. This is the moment available to you, as the past and future are not—put all you have into it. Use your best crystal for your breakfast orange juice. Use your grandparents' dessert plates for your fruit. Use your engraved stationery for a note to a friend. Spend a night in a nearby inn. Nothing is too good for everyday.

Today is the day. Celebrate it. Make it thrilling. Have a picnic with the children today while the sun is shining brightly. Don't count on the sun tomorrow. Go to the zoo. Ride on the carousel. Fly a kite. Walk on the beach. Dance under the stars. Wear your best nightgown or pajamas tonight; you are still on your honeymoon if you choose to be. Look your best, feel your best, do your best to enjoy yourself now. Who and what are holding you back?

There are many little things we can do to be "at the banquet," even if money is tight. Living a beautiful, happy life is not about spending money but how you spend your life. People are so caught up in *busy-ness* that they are always preparing for something wonderful to happen at a future date rather than capturing the joy in these unrepeatable, fleeting now moments. The best is always what we have today.

Peter and I always say, "Life is short. Let's go." We always have breakfast together to start the day. This is a ritual we look forward to wherever we are. We try to have tea together every afternoon. Whether we visit a nearby art museum, go for a bike ride, attend a religious service, hear a lecture, or do errands, we enjoy doing things together. We go for walks, plant hydrangeas in the garden, read by the fire, bake chocolate chip cookies to share with children. We carve out moments, hours, days, and years of joy by *being* together. Whether we listen to a local jazz band on Sunday afternoons or paint watercolors wherever we travel, the fun is right here where we make it. You can take your child to a park with a waterfall, a bookstore, a library, a playground, or a toy store. Just a ride in the car can be a big adventure to a two-year-old.

The best is here, now, always now.

DO NOT LOOK BACK ON HAPPINESS, OR DREAM OF IT IN THE FUTURE.
YOU ARE ONLY SURE OF TODAY; DO NOT LET YOURSELF
BE CHEATED OUT OF IT.

Henry Ward Beecher

No One Else Really
Knows or Understands

❋

NO HUMAN BEING CAN REALLY UNDERSTAND ANOTHER,
AND NO ONE CAN ARRANGE ANOTHER'S HAPPINESS.

Graham Greene

Your happiness is up to you. No one can know you completely, nor should they. Knowing and understanding yourself is key to trusting yourself. It's your right, responsibility and privilege to make your own decisions. You own what you say yes to, and what you say no to.

Trust your inner voice; your intuition is always with you. The only times I seem to make mistakes are when I'm not confident enough in myself to listen and hear my own truth.

Make the right choices for you, weighing all the circumstances. Try not to put pressure on those closest to you to understand your feelings. Most people seek friends and lovers who "understand" them. This puts a huge burden on loved ones. It isn't fair to them. Your emotional life is complex and ever-changing. It is better to let others love you as you are, but don't have unrealistic expectations of their ability to comprehend you. No one else is you. No one else knows how it feels to *be* you. Don't expect it of others. If you do, you're setting yourself up for disappointment. In your times of despair, no one completely understands.

They can't. Don't ask more of someone than they're capable of giving. Unrealistic expectations of others to know how you feel can cause you to feel alone, isolated, and disconnected from others.

Continue to deepen your understanding of yourself. You know your path. Have conviction that you know what is right from what is wrong for you at the time. Even in victory, in the best of times, those closest to you will not fully know what it took for you to surmount the obstacles. Know that *you* know, that *you* understand, and feel blessed.

Listen to your own good advice. Pat yourself on the back. Living is a courageous act. This is not the work or job of others', but of yours alone, and it goes both ways: You can't know or understand loved ones fully, either. Listen to their stories when they open up to you. Value your intimacy with them. You are being entrusted with their deepest self.

Seek information from others, but limit seeking advice. Use your inner compass. Everyone is on his or her own path, at a different pace and at a different place on his or her journey. Our lover's life is separate from ours; we are like two vertical pillars side by side. If one of us leans too heavily on the other, we both may fall down. Once we're adults, we're on our own. Whatever you need to do, do it. You are the architect and owner of every choice you make. With the privilege of autonomy, there is responsibility.

Saint Francis of Assisi taught us, not to try to be understood, but to understand. Be understanding of others as you evolve into higher states of consciousness, aware of more and more depth of awareness within you. You are on your own, but you are never alone, because you are an intricate part of everything else in the universe. There is no way you can separate yourself from all that is. The universe is not out there somewhere; its guidance is inside you all the time.

You have everything you will ever need for your potential to be fulfilled, for your self-knowledge and personal transformation. Your inner resources increase every day. You have the seeds that can take strong root in life. Cultivate yourself. It's not the job of someone else to know or understand you. Accept this truth and be at peace with it.

I WANT, BY UNDERSTANDING MYSELF, TO UNDERSTAND OTHERS.
I WANT TO BE ALL THAT I AM CAPABLE OF BECOMING.

Katherine Mansfield

Onward and Inward

❋

THE HUMAN SPIRIT IS STRONGER THAN
ANYTHING THAT CAN HAPPEN TO IT.

George C. Scott

As you move onward in your outer world of your five senses, move inward as well, because there are riches there that you've been seeking. Honor your spirit world and spend your natural inheritance wisely. Most people live on the circumference of life. Your true home is in the center of your soul, not in the world of material appearances.

We're here to transform and transcend ourselves. When we cultivate the discipline to dwell in the consciousness of love, we become enlightened. The sun is shining; you just can't always see it from your perspective. I love the feeling of getting on a plane and flying above the clouds into the brilliant light. Going inward is our way to see the light, to experience greater clarity and harmony.

We all spend a great deal of our precious resources (time, energy, and money) taking care of the material aspects of our lives. Because we can see what needs our attention there, we believe it is a high priority. Our outer world is full of static, clutter, and confusion. There seems to be a negative slant to almost everything, and everywhere you go, people's conversations reflect this. You're constantly bombarded with a litany of things to worry about.

You read the newspapers, watch television, listen to the radio, and peruse magazines, learning about terrifying events and horrifying things that could happen to you, your loved ones, and others. In a sensitive person this can cause great anxiety. When you focus on the outer, material, human plane, there is a melancholy tendency to think of loss. You naturally want things to be better. You want to fill up your cup.

Challenge your mind not to fall into the trap of worrying about the worst that could happen. Don't allow negative thoughts to dampen your soul. Turn inward immediately for refreshment and inner peace.

When you go inward, your cup is always more than half full. It is, in fact, more likely brimming over, flowing with new inspiration, new desires, and new energy that summons your life force to thrive. Tell yourself "onward," making a promise that you're going to get through this situation as best you can. Nothing is going to overwhelm you. Inwardly, go and gather strength.

When you go within, you immediately calm down, begin to breathe deeply; you feel back in touch with your center. You feel energized, alive, and connected, not scattered. Many people don't believe they have this vast eternal inward space because it is invisible. Seeing is not believing: what you don't see physically is the most important aspect of your entire being.

Go inward on a daily basis for introspection and self-examination. One of the great benefits of meditation is the clearing of the mind of all "thinking." It cleans out all negative thoughts that, interestingly, seem to keep us always stuck in the past or scurrying toward an unknown future.

Remove yourself from the noise and chatter. Tuck in. Block it all out. Visualize yourself on a beautiful beach, in a paradise garden, or wherever you love to be. You shut your eyes to see the truth. Make yourself a refuge. Tell yourself, "I can ground myself." Here, you're able to put everything in perspective.

Think of your priorities. Focus on all you have. Stay centered. Be still. If you were looking down from the level of total awareness, how important are the things that cause you stress and worry? They are passing, fleeting, and, perhaps, meaningless. Worrying about some future negative possibility is poisonous, blocking you from experiencing the magnificence of this wonderful moment that you will never get back.

Step back, step out of the whirl, step beyond.

THE FAIREST THING WE CAN EXPERIENCE IS THE MYSTERIOUS.
IT IS THE FUNDAMENTAL EMOTION WHICH STANDS AT THE CRADLE
OF TRUE ART AND TRUE SCIENCE. HE WHO KNOWS IT NOT AND CAN
NO LONGER WONDER, CAN NO LONGER FEEL AMAZEMENT, IS AS GOOD
AS DEAD, A SNUFFED-OUT CANDLE.

Albert Einstein

When You Change One Thing,
Feel Free to Rethink Everything

※

THE TRUE WISDOM IS TO BE ALWAYS SEASONABLE,
AND TO CHANGE WITH A GOOD GRACE
IN CHANGING CIRCUMSTANCES.

Robert Louis Stevenson

When I was a young interior decorator, I realized how easily the dynamics of a space change with the addition or subtraction of just one object. I was trained never to freshen up one fabric in a room without being prepared to have to redo everything because the new made the old look tired.

Everything is intimately connected, one thing to another. We have to think of the small in the big. One thing certainly leads to another. We have to keep an open mind. Life is as fluid as a babbling brook. The energy keeps flowing without end. Being flexible, being able to adapt well to change in changing circumstances is the best way to navigate the unknown, uncharted future.

See a single change as an opportunity for many new beginnings. If your children have left home, sell the big house with all its maintenance needs and buy a condominium near the beach or an apartment downtown near the places you love to visit.

Any abrupt ending—an airline flight canceled that ruins a vacation, even getting fired—is an opportunity to start anew and do something different. Take it as a signal to start fresh.

If you discover that you really love the color blue, change your bedroom colors to bring you greater happiness. Painting the ceiling pale blue and buying a new set of blue-and-white sheets can make a huge difference in your mood and outlook. If you'd always taken an inexpensive, all-inclusive vacation in Barbados and the hotel has now gone out of business, consider other islands where you can get the same inexpensive package plan.

If you've been a longtime employee at a firm that was bought by a mega-rival company and you lose your job, rethink what you really want to do at this chapter in your life. You may choose to do some freelance consulting or teach a class on your expertise. When your grown daughter falls in love, it is natural for her to distance herself from you. She won't call home or come home as often. Rather than waiting by the telephone for her call, begin to do some things you hadn't focused on before: take some evening art classes or learn to tap dance. Your daughter needs her space, and you need to have your own life.

When water rushes toward a rock, it doesn't stop, but continues traveling around the obstruction. Things will never work out exactly the way you want them to. If you are rigid and cannot see fresh possibilities, you will be frustrated at every detour. A rigid, inflexible branch of an oak tree snaps off in a hurricane.

Follow the old Chinese saying from the *Tao Te Ching*: "Bend and be straight." Resist resistance. Certain life changes require looking freshly at the other areas of your life. Look at the picture of your life from the highest perspective. Then look at your individual choices, the ways you take charge to create the best possible life for yourself.

You are the one who makes these life changes. You choose the best possible option. When I decided to give up my midtown office and go back to working from home, I brought two assistants with me. Immediately, I felt a great loss of privacy. Someone was always seated at my desk in what had been my cozy writing room. After these helpers eventually quit, I didn't replace them. I now have free range of the space, and my part-time administrative assistant works from her home office.

There will be many surprises, new adventures, and new ways of shaping each chapter of your life. Be open-minded and elastic.

TO EXIST IS TO CHANGE, TO CHANGE IS TO MATURE, TO MATURE IS TO GO ON CREATING ONESELF ENDLESSLY.

Henri Bergson

Stick to Your Plan

*

TO KNOW WHAT HAS TO BE DONE, THEN DO IT, COMPRISES
THE WHOLE PHILOSOPHY OF PRACTICAL LIFE.

Sir William Osler

Nothing great is ever accomplished without plans and perseverance. If there is something you have a strong desire to accomplish, you owe it to yourself to stay focused. When I was a young mother with a demanding design career, I decided to write a book. In order to accomplish this goal, I made a pact with myself to get up at five o'clock seven mornings a week to write. This way I could look forward to two pure hours every new day. While it took seven years of hard work before my first book was published, I eventually reached my goal.

There will never be any time that is "free." You have to claim specific hours to have all to yourself. Make a date with this most important person in your life—you—and show up. Set strong boundaries. Remove yourself entirely from your usual environment if necessary. I went to a nearby library to write in order to get away from being the center of our family life. Make it clear that you need to be alone in order to concentrate.

Stick to your plan in every aspect of your life. How important is it to you to have your creative energies manifest into something tangible that you are proud of? If you make a commitment to lose weight, be strict at a restaurant and don't let the waiter tempt you with free desserts. To fulfill your goal to stay healthy and fit, decide the night before what time you're going to the gym. Go.

When people call you with work-related problems, don't be always available to them, otherwise your plans grind to a halt. You can't live from project crisis to project crisis and accomplish your goals. You are legitimately occupied, just like a surgeon in the operating room. You must take your work seriously, organizing your day for focused time. You need to allot time to begin new projects in addition to completing the ones you're working on.

If you enjoy taking vacations with your family, this is your sacred time. Don't tell too many people where you're going or when. Chances are that someone will want to join you. This is not what you planned. Plan a weekend off alone: hire a babysitter, order your train tickets, reserve a room at the inn, and go. Make regular playdates with your children.

Have the confidence to stick with your plan. Know what makes you the most comfortable. Be resolute. Do it. When I have a work plan, I feel disrupted if some outside circumstance blocks me from the time I have set for accomplishing my goals. Remind yourself that if you lose your discipline and focus by giving in to outer demands, you will feel frustrated. Be decisive. Make up your mind. Stick to your guns unless there is a good reason for you to change your schedule. Write down the truly important reasons that would make you deviate from your prearranged schedule. Existentialism works well in the trenches of life; its maxim is "No excuses." Try to be strong about your choice to accomplish your goals. Pride yourself on being inner-directed and proactive, not reactive.

Pay attention to your inner distractions: what diverts your mind from completely focusing your attention? We have so many ways of distracting ourselves, making excuses, doing other things first. So many of us start things we don't finish. If you wander away from your plan, you might destroy the whole project. Don't lose the flow of your momentum.

No one is out to deliberately keep you from achieving your objectives, but loved ones and others will interrupt you and tax your time. It is noble to cultivate and exercise discipline. Make it a habit to stick to your plan. The responsibility for making the personal commitment to carve out time and space for yourself and your goals is in your hands.

As you plan daily goals, you should also arrange several times in your day to meditate, to study, to think through your life's direction, as you're developing and sticking to your philosophy of living.

The good news is you can never be in two places at a time. You choose.

I DO NOT TRY TO DANCE BETTER THAN ANYONE ELSE.
I ONLY TRY TO DANCE BETTER THAN MYSELF.

Mikhail Baryshnikov

Don't See People for How They Could Be, but as They Really Are

WE LIVE IN A FANTASY WORLD, A WORLD OF ILLUSION.
THE GREAT TASK IN LIFE IS TO FIND REALITY.

Lewis Mumford

In Greek mythology, the cruel king of Corinth, Sisyphus, was condemned forever to roll a huge stone up a hill in Hades only to have it roll down again upon nearing the top. Trying to see people, not as they are, but as they could become, fully actualized, is as defeating as rolling a huge stone uphill, only to have it roll down. We have to learn to accept people as they really are. We can't force someone to grow into their higher self. No one likes to be told what to do, or how to shape up.

We know others by intuition. It is not up to us to judge others, to size them up, reform them, or figure them out. This is not your job. A research doctor once told me that you cannot change anyone else more than about five percent. Rather than trying to reform others, we should concentrate on our own inner work. This is our job. We can change ourselves fifty percent, studies show. We can provide unconditional love no matter where others are emotionally and spiritually. If someone has bad character, it is not your responsibility to reform him or her. That job belongs to them.

The truth is the truth. My mistakes in judgment have been when I've given someone the benefit of the doubt. When we fool ourselves into unrealistic expectations of others, we can end up in trouble. When I was young, I thought that I could change people. I believed I could make someone love me. I felt I had the power to make someone happy. I would confront their negative energy. Being captain of the cheerleading team in high school didn't produce a single winning football game. Sis! Boom! Bah! We had a great group of acrobatic cheerleaders, but the guys out on the field were not a winning team.

If our spouse's, a child's, or loved one's shenanigans impinge on us, does loving them mean we can never confront them? How can we strike that balance between acceptance of what people do and drawing boundaries so we don't get hurt? How can we avoid being steamrollered or sucked into someone else's dysfunction? How can we accept others while not getting too permissive or too passive?

Don't reward negative behavior. Calmly, compassionately, lovingly let the person who is misbehaving know that their behavior is unacceptable, that you choose not to be around this toxic atmosphere. Rather than engaging in an argument, announce that you are going for a walk because you need to be by yourself. People who are out of line often feel guilty and may become defensive. They need space to move off their position. You also can't reason with people who have had too much to drink. Take immediate steps to ensure their (and your) safety. The next day you can gently announce that you will never drive with anyone who drinks and drives.

Offer encouragement, love, and a good example, and let others be. You have your hands full. The universe will help them, through appropriate teachers, when they're ready to learn. Continue to concentrate on your inner work and growth. Everyone eventually chooses for themselves how high they will dare to fly.

Believe in their potential. Believe in their best. But accept others as they really are.

EVEN GREATER THAN FAITH AND HOPE IS THE ABILITY
AND WILLINGNESS TO CULTIVATE LOVE. HOW DO WE CULTIVATE LOVE?
WE CAN LET GO OF IMPULSES TO JUDGE OTHERS.
WE CAN REFUSE TO FEEL GOOD ABOUT THE MISTAKES
OR SUFFERINGS OF ANYONE.
WE CAN LIVE THE LESSONS OF KINDNESS. . . .
WE CAN CHOOSE LOVE WHEREVER AND WHENEVER WE
ARE BY SIMPLY MAKING THAT CHOICE.

Pierre Teilhard de Chardin

There Is No Security Except Within Us

❋

ONLY IN GROWTH, REFORM, AND CHANGE, PARADOXICALLY ENOUGH,
IS TRUE SECURITY TO BE FOUND.

Anne Morrow Lindbergh

The only true security is what is inside us. Outside circumstances are often outside our control. Attend to things you can control, but don't go around single-handedly trying to right every wrong. You can't take on the world. There are certain situations you have to give over to the universe. The security within us gives us the freedom to move about with a sense of inner peace, faith, and hope. Rather than being fearful of the future and seeking security, think instead of opportunity.

We don't have to be thrown off by what is happening all around us. We should keep focused on all the good in our lives. Your well-being is cultivated by you, thought by thought, hour by hour. When you have a prepared mind, you are in control of your mood and attitude. You never have to be afraid of life.

The only real way to calm your fears, gain in faith, and grow more hopeful is to think about your own blessings. Know, now and always, that all is well and that well-being is your natural state.

Relying on outside "security" can be comforting, but is probably no

122 ❋ Alexandra Stoddard

more secure than building a sand castle on the beach at high tide. You could lose your money in risky technology investments. You could lose your job when the company where you work downsizes. Friends and colleagues could betray you. Your home could be devastated by a tornado. There is no guarantee of safety. By looking at all the good you are experiencing in the present moment, you will not make the mistake of taking your good fortune for granted. Live your life knowing that peace of mind, harmony, balance, and love are your true security.

There have been dozens of times when I've been able to hold steady through chaotic situations. In each case I've done so by calming myself within. Everyone has to find their own method that works best for them. I meditate. I work on my breathing. After several minutes of focusing on my breathing in and out, I repeat my mantra, "Love and live happy." I transport myself to the beauty of nature; through visualization techniques I'm able to envision a beautiful garden. I often go in my mind to my mother's garden the day I became aware of beauty when I was three years old. I feel the sun on my back. I listen to the wind rustling the leaves in the trees. I hear the birds singing. I see the butterflies dancing. I hear the buzzing of the bees. I see the magnificent colors. I feel a great inner peace.

I'm able to achieve and maintain this serenity in every conceivable circumstance. Once you know that you can produce this inner calm by being one hundred percent in the moment, being mindful about every thought, feeling, and sensation you're having, you begin to feel secure. Don't wait for a crisis and hope for this inner peace. Practice meditation in your daily life as a habit and a discipline so that this powerful inner strength and courage is there to help you remain calm during the storms of life. When we contemplate life from the highest conscious level, we're more able to see things in perspective. A friend told me she was able to keep her equilibrium when her father was diagnosed with prostate cancer by writing a poem to and for him every morning, before her hectic day of caring for three children began.

What goes on around you is not nearly as important as what goes on inside of you. You have the key to open the door to this most sacred secure place. Turn the lock. You're safe and free.

THERE IS NO SECURITY ON THIS EARTH. ONLY OPPORTUNITY.

General Douglas MacArthur

Exercise the Vocabulary of Thanks and Appreciation

❋

A HUNDRED TIMES EVERY DAY I REMIND MYSELF THAT
MY INNER AND OUTER LIFE DEPEND ON THE LABORS OF OTHER MEN, LIV-
ING AND DEAD, AND THAT I MUST EXERT MYSELF IN ORDER
TO GIVE IN THE SAME MEASURE AS I HAVE RECEIVED
AND AM STILL RECEIVING.

Albert Einstein

Celebrate people who are in your life—past and present, close by as well as far away. Thank everyone who contributes to your sense of well-being and joy, whether you know them personally or not. Every day, think of all the people who help make your life so rich and rewarding.

We are healthier and happier when we give and receive appreciation and thanks. If you think it would be fun to throw a big party, do it because you want to: enjoy the preparation, all the planning, and then the event. But when your efforts are appreciated, and your friends thank you, it makes you even more glad that you put in all the work.

When you recognize the value and significance of the hundreds of people who continuously do things for you, you expand your love of life, your faith in the genuine goodness of your fellow men and women.

Make it a habit to write generously spirited thank-you notes. They always bring a smile and create an additional bond. Out of the blue, extend a thank-you to someone in your past who helped you shed light on your career path. Never underestimate the significance to others of your loving thoughts and words. I'm touched by the generous spirits of those who come to hear me speak. Some of the letters I receive are heartwarming. We all like to be appreciated.

Grab a piece of paper and scribble down all of the people and things you're appreciative of. There are many. Would your list include mentors, family, supporters, friends, classmates, and partners, as well as architecture, art, design, color, beaches, and books? I'm appreciative for the sunrise each day, for an opportunity to love and be loved, and for the ability to raise my consciousness through study and meditation, through work and free time. The more I give thanks and appreciation, the more my life's experience increases in value.

It's terribly important to thank people, not only for favors done, but also for paid work well done. People tend to think that they don't need to thank others who were "just doing their job." Anyone who has paid for shoddy workmanship knows the value of paid work well done. By recognizing their contribution, when someone goes the extra mile for you, you are recognizing everything it took to do the work they completed—the skill, the compassion, the good planning, and the thought that permeate the work of someone who cares.

When Peter and I needed to have the air conditioners in our apartment repaired, the company representative came quickly and couldn't have been more efficient. When we paid the invoice, we received a note of thanks from the company. It was the best kind of transaction: mutually beneficial, with respect and goodwill all around.

Give thanks and feel good about yourself for honoring the dignity and commitments of others. The more appreciative you are and the more you give thanks, the greater your own abundant joy.

I CONSIDER MY ABILITY TO AROUSE ENTHUSIASM AMONG MEN THE
GREATEST ASSET I POSSESS, AND THE WAY TO DEVELOP THE BEST THAT
IS IN A MAN IS BY APPRECIATION AND ENCOURAGEMENT.

Charles Schwab

Develop the Rhythm of Buffer Time

❋

A DAY AWAY ACTS AS A SPRING TONIC.

Maya Angelou

Studies confirm that even our hearts stop beating—in order to rest—during a twenty-four hour period. Take regular breaks. I call these free times "white spaces"—time, not to be scheduled, but to be used as the spirit moves you.

The buffer time of white spaces is the key to staying connected to our source energy, to living a radiant and full life. Between events, always build in some extra time to use however you choose. When you remove yourself from responsibility, you have time, space, and privacy to fill your own well. You can't continue to give without replenishing your own resources.

If you have a lot of social activities one weekend, spend the next weekend with your husband and children alone. Instead of entertaining friends, have family celebrations. If you're traveling on business to several cities, find a space in your schedule to stay an extra day in one city after your work is finished. Sleep without setting an alarm, enjoy room service, go to a museum, walk about, look around, absorb the freedom before you move on. You need that time to unwind, to take it all in and get your life back to normal.

Blocking out regular prearranged times to do nothing allows you the peace to decide how best to use this free time. You may need a nap, or perhaps you want a massage or time to curl up in a chair and read, or clean a closet, or touch up the picket fence. Never be a slave to an unre-alistically crowded calendar.

Without buffer time, you burn out. Why become worn out, exhausted, and depleted when it is avoidable? Rushing from one activ-ity to another, from one obligation to another duty, often creates long-term stress. Illness can follow constant tension. Throughout every chapter in your life you need a shield, a cushion, from too much stress and pressure. You need to pace yourself well even after happy events, as you need time to appreciate your good fortune. When you fall in love, you need more time to celebrate and integrate this new wonder into your life. You need time to reflect, to absorb what you are feeling, to be thankful.

I think of buffer time as meditation. It allows us to pay attention to our minds, centering us in the precious current moment. Whether we meander in the woods watching the dappling light on our path, write an affirmation in our journal, or window-shop, we are refreshing ourselves with insights and inspiration.

When you are the most challenged, buffer time protects you from becoming discouraged or overwhelmed. You need to feel that you are free to do whatever feels right at the time. Buffer time allows you to keep your perspective, to stay focused on what's really meaningful to you.

TO STRIVE FOR LEISURE AS AN ALTERNATIVE TO WORK
WOULD BE CONSIDERED A COMPLETE MISUNDERSTANDING OF ONE
OF THE BASIC TRUTHS OF HUMAN EXISTENCE, NAMELY, THAT WORK
AND LEISURE ARE COMPLEMENTARY PARTS OF THE SAME LIVING PROCESS
AND CANNOT BE SEPARATED WITHOUT DESTROYING THE JOY
OF WORK AND THE BLISS OF LEISURE.

E. F. Schumacher

Think of Yourself:
By Being Self-Centered,
You May Be Benefiting the World

※

IT IS NOT FROM THE BENEVOLENCE OF THE BUTCHER, THE BREWER,
OR THE BAKER THAT WE EXPECT OUR DINNER, BUT FROM
THEIR REGARD TO THEIR OWN INTEREST.

Adam Smith

This may shock you, but the most important person in your life is you. You are meant to be "full of yourself." Who else can you be full of, if not you? Your life force is your unique energy, your power, your enthusiasm. To think otherwise is wrong. The only person in the universe who has access to your mind is you. This is for you to use to transform your ordinary self into a radiantly happy soul whose goal in life is to share and spread this happiness.

You are here to be as self-centered as is humanly possible. For the most part, you should do what you want to do. Until you understand this principle, you will be blocking your power, disconnecting from your center.

The late Katharine Hepburn was richly endowed with self-confidence, captivating everyone around her with her spirit. If everyone had her inner sureness, chances are the world would be a far more exciting and happy place. She kept illustrating to us that "self is a gift not to be doubted, or squandered or pawned for less than it's worth," as the *New York Times* reported in her obituary.

The ancient Greek philosophers taught us that what makes you feel good is actually good. Quietly, confidently, go about your life doing what excites you. Do your work, do whatever expands you. When you're really having fun, you don't have to tell everyone. Sad but true, people suffer from envy and jealousy. Focus your force on you. Reinforce yourself. Don't look around for the approval of others.

When you are in the habit of thinking of yourself and for yourself, you will develop your exceptionally original mind. Others should accept you on your own terms, or you will not be able to be with them. Remaining true to who you really are and what you are is powerful and all-important to your own growth and understanding. It is not the job of others to be critical of you. Your work is to improve your own attitude and outlook. If you have negative traits, you should be working on them hour by hour.

Refuse to be diminished. Once you feel comfortable centering yourself, not seeking direction from others, you are free. In the beginning, we are totally dependent on others to teach us what we need to know. However, there is a difference between consulting others as part of making up our own mind and letting others tell us what to think. It is never appropriate to let others tell us what we should think or do or who we should be and become. There is a significant difference between having a spiritual guide to help us find our path and worshipping the teacher. Our goal should be self-transformation, not hero worship. When you work so hard that you outgrow the need for your teachers, you become the teacher. When you go beyond what others have taught you, you're now able to pick up where they left off.

The one person you can transform is you. To be self*less* is to lose your core identity, to be *without* self. Can you think of anyone who serves others who has no sense of self? Through loving yourself, you learn to cherish and love others.

You are individual, unique, separate, and different from everyone else. Your self, the "me" in you, is your force for good. You have special talents, gifts you've been given. You have unique skills, perspective, and experiences that empower you to do your unique good in the world. You are pure potential. Through loving your life, you strive to live in such a way that you contribute to the collective whole that is pure, good, and loving.

Do the things that make you feel enthusiastic, that increase your energy. Everything good you give back to the universe comes from your daring to be yourself. Allow real friends to be self-centered as well. True friends should let go and let each other be free.

Read Emerson's "Self-Reliance": "Nothing is at last sacred but the integrity of your own mind." What does this mean to you? Examine the integrity of your mind, your character, your love. Learn to trust yourself to spend your life doing what you believe is important to you. Whenever you rely on your highest consciousness, you will be serving the world well. Believe in your own unique thinking. Be proud that you are self-centered.

WITHOUT SELF-CONFIDENCE WE ARE AS BABES IN THE CRADLE.

Virginia Woolf

Keep Doing
What You're Doing

❋

THE OLDER YOU GET, THE MORE IMPORTANT
IT IS NOT TO ACT YOUR AGE.

Ashleigh Brilliant

Continue to believe in and do what you're doing until you take your last breath. As you become more mature, you will have a wealth of wisdom to impart to the next generation. Find ways to pass along what you know.

Think of your brain as a muscle. Stretch it. Try to continue your important work throughout your final chapters in this world. You have more to contribute than you'll ever be able to comprehend.

Never allow others' lack of knowledge and understanding of who you really are limit you. Someone may look old but actually be vibrantly young at heart. You'll never become old if you continue to express yourself. Take up great, important projects as though you have eternity to complete them. Keep on keeping on.

The microbiologist, author, Pulitzer Prize winner, and contemporary philosopher Dr. René Dubos was writing a book, sitting up in bed listening to a tape of church bells, when he took his last breath. After reading his bestselling book, *A God Within,* in the early 1970s, I became deeply influenced by his belief that enthusiasm is the God Within. Later, I learned that many minds I greatly admired also loved Dr. Dubos, and I had the good fortune of meeting him and forging a friendship. Dr. Dubos's insights helped me shape my book *Living a Beautiful Life.* He told me during our first meeting, "Interior designers tend to complicate everything. People haven't changed much since the Stone Age. We eat, we sleep, and we bathe. We stand up, we sit down, and we lie down." My brain lit up. I decided to structure the book according to our rituals, celebrations, and ceremonies; by ritualizing the smallest details of our daily lives, we give meaning and dignity to our existence.

The former bishop of New York, Paul Moore, preached on peace to a crowded cathedral just weeks before dying of inoperable cancer. Eric Butterworth, the beloved minister of the Unity Movement, wrote his masterful Easter sermon after leaving the hospital a few days before he died. His wife, Olga, read it in Lincoln Center's Avery Fisher Hall on Easter Sunday with a promise that his work would continue. E. B. White's wife, a passionate gardener, was planning her garden just before her death.

Plant trees, both literally and metaphorically. The seeds you sow now will be around for future generations to enjoy. Dig in your garden and be a passionate gardener of life. What you do in your maturity will be your immortality. Thomas Jefferson said he might be an old man but he was a young gardener. Do all the things you loved to do as a child. Fly a kite with your great-grandchildren. Gather seashells on the beach. Blow bubbles. Jump rope. Read the ancient philosophers. Go to lectures. Wisdom isn't possible without a great deal of life's experiences. When you keep on keeping on, you become wise and attain lasting happiness.

Be up and doing things every day. Never stop. Never give in. Never give up. Cultivate your sense of hope and freedom by continuing to learn and grow wiser every day. Don't let anyone snuff out your candle.

The physical body is only a small part of who you are. Your soul will never die.

Be a shining example to others of how productive and rich life can be when you're in your nineties. Write a book, paint pictures, take up photography. Dance, hike, travel. Love. Don't allow anyone to chip away at your spirit. You are sacred and only get better as you mature.

Throughout the entire spectrum of your long, productive life, seek to remain young at heart. That is how you will realize your full potential. Believe in what you're doing and keep doing it. A sage in his late eighties once said with a wink, "My age is none of my business."

REFUSE TO LET AN OLD PERSON MOVE INTO YOUR BODY.

Wayne W. Dyer

Your Soul Is Not for Sale

❊

WE LIVE IN SUCCESSION, IN DIVISION, IN PARTS, IN PARTICLES.
MEANTIME WITHIN MAN IS THE SOUL OF THE WHOLE;
THE WISE SILENCE; THE UNIVERSAL BEAUTY,
TO WHICH EVERY PART AND PARTICLE IS EQUALLY RELATED:
THE ETERNAL ONE.

Emerson

Your soul is the unflagging first principle of your being. It comprises the essential you. It is your nonphysical self, your true nature that shapes your thoughts, actions, and emotions. It is there to be your guide, your constant companion, your spirit world. Your soul is your divinity, and no one has access to it but you.

A friend told me that at a conference about the soul she recently attended, a CEO raised his hand and asked two questions: "How much does a soul weigh?" and "Where is it located?" When Thomas Moore, author of *Care of the Soul,* told him it is "nonmaterial," he stormed out of the crowded auditorium in frustration and disdain.

While it may be impossible to entirely understand your soul, commit to nourishing it or you will lose your way. Our soul needs to be developed throughout our lives. I always think of the trinity that Aristotle taught us: to dwell on what is good, beautiful, and true. I nourish my soul by sharing my happiness with others, by cherishing the good in people, and by finding ways to express loving kindness in my relation-ships. When I think positive thoughts, when I focus on all the good in the world, when I seek and find beauty all around me and cultivate it internally, I'm able to illuminate my individual essence on a regular basis. I feel comfortable with nonphysical realities that cultivate and elevate my soul. Love, faith, hope, happiness, and compassion are all nutrients that heal us, strengthen us, and ultimately make us wise. I read books by wise people whom I respect and believe have expansive eternal souls.

How can we prevent our soul from being diminished? How does it feel when our soul is at stake in a specific situation? When a television producer approached me about hosting my own daily show, I did some soul-searching. I would have to create the show; when I wasn't filming, I'd have to work to develop future shows. When would I be free to write? How could I find time to lecture? Where would I find time to enjoy the flowers? Gardens? Sunlight? Children? Beaches? Color? It became obvious to me that this opportunity wasn't appropriate for me. We must constantly work on developing our soul while at the same time preserving its integrity.

Once I was falsely accused of a wrongdoing by a boss. Rather than letting her get away with her accusation, I stood up for the truth and the charge was dropped. I had a client who was a perfectionist, incapable of liking anything. Nothing was ever right. I was paid for all the work I'd done, but I felt hollow inside receiving money for such an unhappy appraisal. I eventually let go of the client in order to save my soul. Your soul is not for sale.

THERE IS AN ESSENCE OF THE DIVINE IN ALL LIVING THINGS.
AND EACH PERSON IS LITERALLY A MICROCOSM OF THE UNIVERSE.

Gloria Steinem

Have Your Own Independent Financial Advisor

※

EVERYONE HAS A RIGHT TO HIS OWN COURSE OF ACTION.

Molière

A commercial banker friend gave me good advice about handling one's own money. "Keep it," he said. Whether you inherit money or earn it, your money is yours and yours alone. Never be too busy to know just where your money is. No matter how much you think you know about your money, hire your own, independent financial advisor. Having your spouse be your financial advisor could be a conflict of interest. Avoid joint accounts and shared finances with anyone. It can cause trouble and awkward misunderstandings. Keep separate accounts and seek private financial advice. Pay the bill out of your own checking account.

Your money should be in a bank that you select or invested in ways you feel comfortable with and that you understand. Your property, like your money, should be in your name. You must pay attention and know all the details of your finances. You need to make your own inquiries and evaluations. The sole control of your finances is your responsibility.

If, for whatever reason, you are not currently in charge of your finances, use diplomacy to regain control. Send a copy of your joint tax return to your own independent financial advisor. Consider having an audit to assure that your books have been maintained accurately. Have regular reports from your independent financial advisor sent to you.

If some money is split fifty-fifty, divide it up immediately and then decide what you want to do with your portion. If you choose to write a check to your spouse from your account, this is a gift you give. There is truly no such thing as joint money.

Having financial control is important because it is a form of power. Do you feel it is especially important for women? I don't see gender as having anything to do with finances. The amount of money involved is not the issue, either. The principle is to have your own money. Don't be naïve about the care of your own finances. Never be too busy with family obligations to keep a close watch on your money. It is your responsibility.

While I am adamant about having my own money and separate finances, Peter and I have shared in the pleasure of a combined Happiness Fund. Together we vote on how we will draw from this joint account, but the rule remains that these sacred yellow checks can only be written for pleasure: new rosebushes, theater tickets, island vacations, paintings, or romantic meals on the town—never for fixing toilets.

A MAN WHO BOTH SPENDS AND SAVES MONEY IS THE HAPPIEST MAN, BECAUSE HE HAS BOTH ENJOYMENTS.

Samuel Johnson

Don't Feel Guilty About Your Feelings Toward Your Parents, Stepparents, or In-Laws

THERE IS JUST ONE LIFE FOR EACH OF US: OUR OWN.

Euripides

There are going to be people in your life who are not a match for you. We choose our friends; we inherit our families.

Ask yourself, would you want these people as friends? When you are with certain family members, how do you feel after being with them? Don't feel guilty about your answers to these questions. Guilt blocks you from all the good in life. You shouldn't feel responsible for situations that are not in your control. Guilt is a negative emotion that drains us of our positive energy; it is destructive, not constructive. Be gentle on yourself. Don't destroy your own harmony, inner peace, and optimism because of certain people who have access to you.

Don't define yourself by your family. Anytime you let someone get under your skin, it is harmful to *you*. All negative thoughts lower *your* vitality, health, and happiness. Emotionally, be in whatever place you choose to be. Be nonresistant. Don't get drawn into confrontations.

Don't judge. Don't *think* about them. This way your heart can continue to expand in love without having your positive energy sullied. No one can alter your mental state without your permission. You hold the key to your inner chamber. Don't give up this precious key.

Once you have your own family, this *is* your family. Your spouse and your children are your first responsibility. I disagree with those who believe you marry into the entire family. Many of us would never get married if that were the truth, if we were completely honest with ourselves. Unfortunately, our spouse is often part of the problem, letting family intrude, insisting we do more, wanting us to feel differently. A great deal of unnecessary pain is caused by unrealistic expectations and lack of open dialogue to express our concerns. How do we handle unrealistic expectations of others?

There will be special events, occasions when you will be with your extended family. You will not be alone, but among many; you'll have the support of your spouse and children. Set a time frame. Remember that no situation is perfect. Every family has awkwardness. Be kind, compassionate, loving, and true to your higher self. Keep your thoughts in lofty places. Whenever I'm with a difficult family member, I try to think of one good thing about him or her. I dwell on that positive thought.

Because there is no sure way to change another person, you should never succumb to feeling guilty that you choose not to spend too much time together. When someone is acting ignorantly out of false beliefs, offer encouragement, cherish their potential. All transformation derives from changing one's mind, attitude, and reaction to life's realities.

Family should not cause us to suffer pain and anxiety. We have to find constructive ways to balance our family's needs with our own. We may have to care for ailing relatives, attend gatherings we'd rather not attend. Try to balance these necessary obligations while steering clear of unnecessary ones. Don't let your family lean on you without your consent. Remain clear that you want true lasting happiness for yourself and that you want to spread this positive energy to others.

THE MORE COHERENT THE FAMILY, THE MORE FIERCELY IT DEFENDS
ITSELF AGAINST INTRUDERS, WHICH IS WHAT YOU ARE. EVEN THOUGH
YOU'RE SMOOTH AND GOOD WITH PEOPLE, YOU SIMPLY DON'T SPEAK
THEIR LANGUAGE, WHICH THEY HAVE BEEN BUSY MAKING PRIVATE FOR
THE PAST TWENTY-FIVE YEARS. YOU MIGHT DO WELL TO REMEMBER
ELEANOR ROOSEVELT'S WISDOM THAT NOBODY CAN INSULT YOU
WITHOUT YOUR PERMISSION.

Hugh O'Neill

Find a Way to Share Your Gifts

✳

GIVE WHAT YOU HAVE. TO SOMEONE, IT MAY BE BETTER
THAN YOU DARE TO THINK.

Longfellow

I owe my life to so many people who have taken me under their wings. I, for the most part, remain a humble apprentice. I'm forever a beginner, a learner, a student. I've been fortunate to spend countless hours in the presence of accomplished people. They enthusiastically continue to encourage me. Many of my mentors have been there for me since early childhood.

I would not be a writer if a senior editor at *Reader's Digest* hadn't asked me to dance with him at a poolside party in Fairfield, Connecticut, in the 1960s. "I see you under a tree writing when you're not playing tennis, Sandie. I'm a writer, too." I admitted I was struggling to become a writer. After the dance he handed me his business card, "If there is ever anything I can do to help you, please give me a call," he said. And I did.

My art history teacher at boarding school saw a spark in me and encouraged me to follow my passion to pursue a design career. Phyl Gardner lived the spirit of art. I spent happy hours with her in her studio designing wallpaper and fabric. Her belief in me helped me to follow my dream to have a career in interior design. My mother and godmother were both mentors to me because they were self-trained interior decorators and believed in the importance of having a formal education in design.

Many others have shared their gifts with me. My spiritual guide, John Bowen Coburn, a friend of my aunt, Ruth Elizabeth Johns, exposed me to the world's religions, helping me to expand my beliefs and understanding.

Spread your message and wisdom. Hire summer interns at your firm, give talks at high schools, or coach Little League: young people are starved for heroes. I enjoy speaking at writers' conferences because I'm in a room full of aspiring writers who cling to every word. They fill notebooks full of affirmations and questions. A friend from Oklahoma City participates in a mentor program, spending time with a second-grade student once a week, helping with homework and doing fun projects together.

Take on a bright young protégé. Just imagine, decades later this student will be a teacher and a mentor as well. People who are successful and passionate should share their gifts. Give your time in ways that remind you why you love what you do.

DEVELOP INTEREST IN LIFE AS YOU SEE IT;
IN PEOPLE, THINGS, LITERATURE, MUSIC—THE WORLD IS SO RICH,
SIMPLY THROBBING WITH RICH TREASURES, BEAUTIFUL SOULS,
AND INTERESTING PEOPLE.

Henry Miller

Embrace Change

✻

YOU CAN NEVER STEP IN THE SAME RIVER TWICE.

Heraclitus

Nothing in our dynamic universe ever stays the same. Stability, para-doxically, is based on unending change. The capacity to adapt to change is a sign of emotional health and intelligence—without it we cannot grow.

The more flexible you are, the more you'll be open to change in any and all circumstances. The core of the Buddha's teachings is the imper-manence of all things. See everything as it is—not as it was or could be. Nothing lasts, good or bad. You never know: it sometimes takes only one second for everything to change. Life is full of unknowns we can't prepare for in advance. We must deal in the present with whatever hap-pens, when it happens.

Embracing impermanence makes all of our relationships more mean-ingful. Life is sacred. What we have now will never be the same again. Each moment has a life of its own. Moment by moment, life changes. We can thrive by staying centered on the present while also being pre-pared, by embracing change, for the future. Be alert to subtle changes in your body, in your mind, in the weather, and in the environment. Respond and accept them as they come.

You're here now. Make the most of what happens and be happy. Join in. You're in the swing, in the thick of life. Embrace it with both arms and a huge heart. Plato taught us not to fear change. The more you know and the more you experience, the less you should fear. You have the capacity to be courageous in handling whatever troubles come your way.

How can you keep this resilience when really bad changes happen? You can recover and adjust easily when you have the understanding that life is made up of ups and downs. You have the inner resources to accept what you cannot change.

Let your life unfold. You are happening today. Don't try to freeze the moment when everything is peaceful and you're happy. Live the moment intensely. When you have one new insight, you are transformed, forever changed, and cannot go back to where you were before this raising of your consciousness. Concentrate on your growth. Each day, embrace new considerations in your thinking. As situations continuously change, rethink everything. Everything is now new.

Trust that life gets better and better and better. The more you grow in love and compassion for others, the more radiantly happy you will become.

TIME IS LIKE A RIVER OF FLEETING EVENTS
AND ITS CURRENT IS STRONG.

Marcus Aurelius

Listen to the Wisdom of Your Body

✤

You are a nonphysical being, temporarily in a physical body. Your body is your sacred temple. Health is internal balance. Radiant health is or should be our true nature. It is more normal to feel well than it is to feel bad. Your challenge is to take good care of yourself and maintain your wellness throughout the course of a long, happy life.

Happiness is imperative to a healthy life. Honor the strong interaction between your healthy mind and your healthy body. Beware of negative thoughts and constant stress that can harm your immune system. Many medical experts believe as I do: When you think negative thoughts, you may be more susceptible to illness, disease, and injuries. Learning to manage stress is one of the most important considerations in maintaining health.

Work on yourself. Begin by training your mind to think positively.

Care well for yourself. Increase your movements: walk more. Try to get a little more sleep. Take extra care of your nutritional needs. Eat a little of everything. Your mind and body appreciate variety. Believe that you are attracted to only what is good and good for you. Believe that your body will be right there helping you accomplish your goals, and give it the care it needs to do so.

In most normal cases, the body heals on its own if it is given time. A family doctor once suggested to us never to stay in bed all day when we didn't feel well. He suggested we dress and move around, but take naps when we felt tired. When you take to your bed for long periods, it weakens you. If you become ill, keep your mind occupied doing what-ever feels good that is also good for you. There is always an emotional component to illness. Your thoughts must remain positive in order for the healing process to work. Rent funny movies. Distract yourself doing something you enjoy. Get out of its way so the body can work its magic.

Peter and I make a conscious effort to rest and recuperate when we are on the road. We catch up on our sleep whenever time permits. We take walks in order to feel invigorated, and we read and spend hours in quiet lulls between media appearances, lectures, and book signings. Being alone together after being in crowds is healing for us. I remember returning to a hotel in Philadelphia late one afternoon just hours before flying to Chicago to be on *Oprah*. We had been on location all day and night. We hadn't eaten. We were sleep deprived. We took hot baths. I lit a candle. We ate a healthy meal and had a nap. Then off we went to the airport. I slept on the plane and arrived refreshed and ready for the show.

No matter how mentally resolute and self-caring we try to be, we may become seriously ill or sustain injuries. If this happens, we need to face our situation, embrace the reality, make necessary decisions, and take steps to be as happy as humanly possible.

I believe we also can benefit from cultivating an expanded definition of health. If health embraces both physical and mental realms, we can use one to enhance the other. Someone who suffers from depression can exercise regularly and, by taking excellent physical care, may ease the illness. Someone who has an incurable illness can meditate regularly and practice mindfulness, living intensely in the moment. Both may reduce pain and help foster inner peace and contentment. The more serious the health issues, the more disciplined one needs to be to focus on the nonphysical aspects of life that give us its rich meaning. It is through difficulties and challenges that we're able to transcend ourselves, cultivating love, patience, kindness, and wisdom and true happiness.

After Peter fell and had emergency knee surgery, he intuitively realized he was more than his physical handicap. The rest of his essence was whole and well. As his knee was healing, he was in pain but was able to think about other people and other things while pursuing every aspect of the rehabilitation process. He tired easily, but worked hard to do his exercises. He distracted himself from the pain by reading biographies of great thinkers he admired. He also listened to inspirational tapes and enjoyed having the time to listen to favorite classical music.

Joy is emotional therapy. You need to have belly laughter. When we laugh, we relax our body. We let go of stress and strain. Health is, in this sense, a laughing matter. Listen to the wisdom of your body when you are happy. How do you feel? Do you feel light, open, and loving? What thoughts and emotions produce this positive mental and physical state? What do you need to do to stay this way? When you are in tune with your body and have control over your mind, you are on the road to being healthier.

You can be ill but still be in tune with your body's needs and, therefore, be "healthy." Health in this broader sense is not always the absence of physical illness or pain; it can be inner lasting happiness that is not based on outer circumstances but is cultivated by us and nurtured by sharing happiness and love with others.

THERE IS A VITALITY, A LIFE FORCE, AN ENERGY, A QUICKENING,
THAT IS TRANSLATED THROUGH YOU INTO ACTION, AND BECAUSE THERE
IS ONLY ONE OF YOU IN ALL TIME, THIS EXPRESSION IS UNIQUE.
AND IF YOU BLOCK IT, IT WILL NEVER EXIST THROUGH ANY OTHER
MEDIUM AND WILL BE LOST.

Martha Graham

Finish Up Strong

❋

ACTION SPRINGS NOT FROM THOUGHT, BUT FROM
A READINESS FOR RESPONSIBILITY.

Dietrich Bonhoeffer

Just as death of the human body is part of the life process, so finishing what you begin completes the cycle of beginning to bring something into existence to then manifesting it. You give something tangible to the universe with the completion of a project. Without your finishing the article, the book, the poem, the painting, or the symphony, chances are the world will never benefit. As a general principle, finish what you start as long as you live.

There is a difference between finishing and finishing strong. When you've stayed your course, given the project your full energy, and followed through to the best of your ability, you've finished up strong. Saying, "the end" will have force and honesty. Now you're free to begin again.

Don't do just what is expected of you. Do what you know will make a difference. A surgeon friend, Charles Larkin, goes to his patients' beds in the recovery room when they are still under anesthetic. He whispers, "The surgery was a huge success. You are ready to go home now. You're in great shape." He also prays for his patients. The power of positive energy!

We're meant to give back to the world using our powerful gifts as cocreators of manmade things—food, houses, gardens, paintings, furniture, books, music, and babies. This has been a core principle of life since the beginning. Some people are afraid to even begin a noble act because they're concerned they won't be able to accomplish it. Others are fearful to finish anything because they don't have the confidence that what they produced is good enough. Don't quit. Be tenacious to the end. Overcome whatever obstacles stand in your way. Perseverance is the central ingredient of success, as sages have recognized.

You deserve nothing less than a triumphant ending. Whenever you start something and don't finish it, do some soul searching. Remind yourself of your goals as well as your time frame for accomplishing them. Identify and analyze the obstacles, and concentrate on eliminating them, or at least circumventing them like water flowing around a boulder. This formula allows for completion of the job on time. When we can count on ourselves, we free others to be able to rely on us also. Whenever we help ourselves, we are benefiting the world.

To help you stay on track, review why a given project is important to you. Every night before I fall asleep I review my commitment to whatever it is I want to finish. In this way I influence my subconscious mind to help me help myself to complete the work. When a project is stalled, ask yourself, what has changed? What makes you flag? When your thoughts are full of excuses, objectively analyze why you have lost interest.

Give yourself a pep talk on the merits of your original choice to bring something constructive to fruition. Tell yourself that this is a contribution to the world, a way of serving others, helping to spread peace of mind and happiness. It always makes us feel better to accomplish what we set out to do. It reinforces our confidence. The best way to stay confident is by rigorous discipline. Train your mind not to make excuses.

Remind yourself that you are trying your best. Develop a procedure that allows you to observe your accomplishments, day by day.

Break up the whole process into manageable parts so that you become realistic about time management, always being able to move a project forward, no matter what your time allows. By understanding that everything takes longer than expected and that when you are enthusiastic and passionate, you will want to go the extra mile, after analyzing what has to be done, you'll allot enough time to complete it.

Sit down. Make no excuses. You are responsible. You will learn what you need to know by doing the work. No matter what you don't know, you'll have the discipline to find out how to proceed. Your vision is the force that culminates in a strong finish. If something isn't right, you are free to redo it. Put it out there. Accomplishing a project is a reward in itself.

When one works in a team, sometimes others keep a project from being finished, or it is finished poorly. I remember a painful experience when I submitted a book under contract the day it was due. The editor didn't edit it for six months, so everyone had to scramble at the eleventh hour to get the book published on time. When other people create sloppiness or keep you from accomplishing your task, it reflects badly on you. How do we keep our own integrity when this happens? Should we try to move the person or team to greater focus and excellence?

People tend to take on more work than they can handle well from start to finish. Some of their projects are shoved under the rug or put on the back burner. Or they lose interest. They move on to other things. When they lose their focus, and the situation directly involves you, deal with the problem directly. Exercise damage control. If a project has flaws, stay on top of it. Oversee the stages along the way. *Check in and check up* is a good working mantra.

From the very beginning of a team undertaking, remind yourself that

158 ❋ Alexandra Stoddard

this is your baby. This is something you care deeply about. Don't make the mistake of waiting until you run into obstacles or disloyalties. Sincerely, with humility, anticipate obstacles and offer encouragement and assistance. You may learn that others share your concerns. Try not to push against anything or anyone. Hold the project up as something bigger than the circumstances that are keeping it from finishing strong. You keep your eye on the ball—the schedule, the details that add up to quality—in order to exercise damage control.

Attempt to draw from a difficult situation the best possible outcome, for the benefit of everyone concerned. To keep yourself on your course, ask yourself, do I care? Why is this important? Who am I benefiting by finishing? Do I believe this work makes a difference to others? Does this project excite me?

What is the significance of failure? Is a failure absolute, or can the project be salvaged? If there is something you can do, save the project from destruction. Start again. Try a different tack; the wind is always fluctuating. You may be ahead of your time or you could be behind the times, but stay open and determine if your failure is irrevocable. When a situation is utterly hopeless, don't stubbornly push ahead through the sand. Sometimes in life we should walk away from things we've taken on and cannot finish. We may have discovered that something we started is wrong for us and be forced to let go, to move on.

I have respect for the writer who halfway through a book under contract finds that he doesn't have the necessary fire in his belly to finish writing it and returns the advance to his publisher. I honor anyone who has searched her conscience and is willing to admit that her marriage is empty and seeks a divorce. These huge choices are extremely painful—and not to be taken lightly. But the expression "there are many ways of skinning a cat" can also be applied to failure. Transform your failure into success by finding another way to express yourself.

Ask to take an exam over again until you pass. Persuade the people involved to let you try again. Conversely, step back and reevaluate your situation. Don't push too hard. Maybe you are taking too many courses in medical school. Perhaps you should spread things out, live a more balanced life, and take an extra year to absorb the material. A minister who was pushing too hard to complete his studies found that he got sick on his breaks in between semesters. He preached a sermon, "Whether You Like It or Not," about balance—not being so focused now on finishing but on paying attention to the joy in the step-by-step process.

Be willing to admit your mistake, no matter how well-meaning your motives. We can't do it all instantly. Whether you push yourself too hard, end a relationship, or decide to quit a job, explore, seek advice, think things through, try again, and remember that if your mission is worthwhile, never give up. Finishing up strong is active virtue. Be strong to the end. There is wisdom in accomplishing your work. As Henry Wadsworth Longfellow said, "Great is the art of beginning, but greater the art is of ending."

Unfinished acts, thoughts, and ideas stay with us, blocking and haunting us. Persistent vision, focus, and commitment are the basis of your heroic determination to finish up strong.

DO YOU KNOW WHAT A BIG SHOT IS?

A LITTLE SHOT WHO KEEPS ON SHOOTING.

Norman Vincent Peale

Love Your Own Company

✻

WHAT A COMMENTARY ON CIVILIZATION, WHEN BEING ALONE IS
CONSIDERED SUSPECT; WHEN ONE HAS TO APOLOGIZE FOR IT,
MAKE EXCUSES, HIDE THE FACT THAT ONE PRACTICES IT . . .
LIKE A SECRET VICE.

Anne Morrow Lindbergh

We become hollow inside when we don't balance our busy lives with time alone to be introspective. We need to be alone in order to meditate, pray, study, train, and purify our mind. Fondness for others, love, and understanding begin with your self-love. Make regular appointments with yourself. We all need ample time to think things through, to clarify our feelings about ourselves, our work, our loved ones, and others.

When you love your own company, you are wealthy. The joy and fascination of choosing to be alone has been understated and misunderstood. The pleasures of alone time have great merits. Whether you enjoy a solitary retreat, spend a weekend at home alone, go for a long walk on a deserted beach, or spend time ironing, you're in what I call "the swing" of who you really are. There are fewer distractions when you carry on a dialogue with yourself.

Ever since I was a baby, I've loved my own company. My mother told me I played in the playpen for hours alone, content. I think I owe my happiness to my solitary times—in the garden, puttering around the house, sitting at the Point watching the boats come and go, sitting at my desk, being *present*. All inner peace, creativity, and personal growth come from our ability to think our thoughts, to concentrate, and to love our own company.

How can we find ways not only to love our own company but to cultivate freedom, independence, and self-reflection amidst a demanding life? How do we balance our inner illumination with our outer stimulation?

Express to loved ones your need to be alone. I have an expression, "I need some Zen time." Who can want to spoil your time alone? If you have toddlers, hide from them when you have a babysitter. Have a secret office in the attic or a favorite spot where you love to go to be alone, where the energy is powerful, where you can go alone and feel truly united.

Quietly get up earlier than your family. If you have an infant, this may not be possible, but that stage lasts only a few short months. The principle is solid. When you acknowledge that you need time to do your spiritual practice *every* day, you will be able to seek and find time to love your own company. Be flexible: it may be when the baby finally goes to sleep, or your spouse goes off to do errands or on a fishing trip, or when the girls are away on a sleepover.

Develop what I like to call *solitude for two*. You can turn inward in silent meditation when you are in the presence of a loved one. Someone once said that it is wonderful to be alone but to be in the company of someone with whom to enjoy it. We can be together physically as we enjoy the space between us.

When you love being alone, you will never feel lonely wherever your life leads you. Never deprive yourself of generous amounts of time to appreciate yourself, by yourself.

LIFE IS WHAT WE MAKE IT, ALWAYS HAS BEEN, ALWAYS WILL BE.

Grandma Moses

Remember That People Are Funny About Money

✳

THE SOVEREIGN ABILITY CONSISTS IN KNOWING
THOROUGHLY THE VALUE OF THINGS.

La Rochefoucauld

Don't assume everyone is as responsible about money as you are. Be careful in all your financial transactions. Put everything in writing. Don't keep money or records lying around for people to see. You can never be too meticulous when you are dealing with money.

Don't borrow from family and friends; it's always best to go to a bank for an official loan. Don't lend family and friends money. You are not a bank. Lending a family member money can cause resentment and hostility in both directions. The borrower feels poor while the lender feels either frustrated if the loan is not repaid as promised or burdened with the thought that the family member may return with another request.

Your spouse, parents, and siblings will never spend money exactly the way that you do. You and your spouse may agree what an average bottle of wine should cost, but that doesn't mean you will agree on how much to spend on new houseplants, appliances, furniture, or a hotel stay. If you need a new stove, what if you don't agree with your spouse what model to purchase? While it is unlikely that we will go through life agreeing on all financial matters, we can agree to disagree.

If a new stove really matters to you and you'll be the one doing most of the cooking, maybe you should pay the difference in order to get the stove that you want. Maintain your own value system in spending money in order to live without regrets. If you fall in love with a painting and your spouse doesn't value putting money into something that hangs on the living room wall, you are free to purchase it on your own. Money is a tool. We should try not to let it interfere with our partnerships or our personal happiness.

Be careful about giving others financial advice, especially if it is not asked for. When it is solicited, I am in favor of it; when unsolicited, I am against it. Be open and calmly discuss money matters with your partner, who has a joint interest in the finances. This should be a natural place for compromise. Many people are happier when you lovingly listen to their needs, desires, and thoughts about family financial matters.

It is not wise to discuss money at work. The conversation ends up being about who gets paid how much, creating bad feelings, jealousy, and envy, and causing morale to suffer. Studies show that people can be happy with their raise, their bonus, their promotion, or their profit sharing until they learn that a coworker was given more. When I went to work for McMillen, Inc., in 1963, the legendary interior design firm that Mrs. Brown founded in 1924, I was informed by the office manager that there was a firm rule that salary and finances were not to be discussed within the company. Everyone was paid appropriately. An independently wealthy person, for example, was often paid less than someone who relied on her salary to maintain her standard of living.

We all want to be judged for who we are, not by what we can earn or how we choose to spend or not to spend our money. If you discuss money with your friends, it is apt to be misinterpreted. Exercise discretion out of decency. Keep your dignity. Never talk about money. Money is personal. It is no one else's business. It is vulgar to discuss money in the same way it is to talk about sexual union.

In money matters among friends who socialize by going out, entertaining and traveling together, you can't always keep the balance even. There will be inequality among friends' financial resources. Be yourself. Put yourself in your friend's place. Allow a friend to spend more money on an occasion than you can afford to reciprocate.

I have many friends I enjoy taking to restaurants. Some of my friends have us over for a delicious meal in their home. It is never wise to overspend just to keep up with friends who have more resources than you do. If you can't meet them for dinner out, perhaps you can join your friends for a glass of wine or dessert, or meet for tea. You don't have to participate in everything. Sometimes it will be appropriate to say that you cannot attend. We all know the joy of paying for friends. Let them give to us on their own terms even if the expense is more than our resources allow for us to return the kindness. Try not to let an imbalance of resources interfere with genuine friendships. Your love for each other is your true wealth, and this richness is far more important and rare than anything money can buy. When you exercise loving kindness, you will want to make your friends feel comfortable.

Either extreme of cheapness or extravagance can offend any of us. But when it comes to money, we cannot all meet in the middle. We must stand by our own value systems, keeping them private but keeping them true. Don't feel pressure to spend less on this or invest more in that because somebody else does.

THE HOLY PASSION OF FRIENDSHIP IS OF SO SWEET AND STEADY AND LOYAL AND ENDURING A NATURE THAT IT WILL LAST THROUGH A WHOLE LIFETIME, IF NOT ASKED TO LEND MONEY.

Mark Twain

Do Your Best
and Leave the Rest

❊

WE SHOULD NOT LET OUR FEARS HOLD US BACK
FROM PURSUING OUR HOPES.

John F. Kennedy

All that is ever asked of you is that you do your best. Stay centered, knowing that you are well. Good things come to you because you are decent—yes, noble. And remember that you are also divine in potential. You have the seeds of greatness.

Focus on what you choose to do and on projects and commitments that you are proud to be a part of. Believe in yourself every step of the way. Loving yourself, your life, and others is the wisest way to be at our best in order to do our best.

You can never do more than give life your best. Use all your energy constructively. When you are faced with an obstacle, use it as a way to strengthen your spiritual progress. Instead of getting angry, practice patience. Instead of blaming others, take personal responsibility. Rather than being fearful and worrying about the future, stay focused on giving your all to the present moment. By training your mind to think positively, looking for the best ways to overcome adversities, thinking about all the ways you can be useful to others, you will avoid the suffering of wondering whether you have done all you reasonably can to repair a negative situation. When your conscience is clear and calm, you will remain happy.

When you are dealing with highly critical people who are never satisfied—your boss, clients, or relatives—try to keep your mind and breathing steady. Let challenging people be your teachers to help you to practice universal compassion, wishing them love and happiness. You are dealing with human beings, and human beings can be wounded, unhappy, and angry. Face the reality, too, that others may be rewarded more for politics than for their performance. Continue to maintain your standards.

If you become bitter or resentful, you are harming yourself and caus-ing unnecessary suffering. When we cultivate the understanding that we are here to transform *our* energy into love, we grow to see that all people can become our teachers in being more loving. The key here is to always be aware of our attitude, our choices, our emotions, and our reac-tions to others.

Cultivating compassion for others in the abstract doesn't work. Reading books about it is helpful, but we have to apply these principles in the trenches of everyday life. No experience, however painful, is ever wasted, because all experiences encourage us to work on ourselves.

Keep your high standards and put your best foot forward. Do all you can, then let go and move on. You are personally responsible for your own life and your life's work. You can't take on all the problems of the universe. You are a wave in the ocean of life. It is not up to you to take upon your shoulders those issues you cannot change. Do what you can the best you can; leave the rest to the universe.

Concentrate on what you want to accomplish and how you want to live. Write a list of things you want to do, in no particular order. Everything is important. Date the list so that you can look at it in a month or two, and you'll be amazed at how clearly you'll then be able to put things in priority. For now, just get your ideas down on paper; for example:

- ❋ Practice meditation
- ❋ Go back to graduate school
- ❋ Have a baby
- ❋ Study metaphysics
- ❋ Keep a journal
- ❋ Live in the moment
- ❋ Go on a spiritual retreat
- ❋ Study world religions
- ❋ Lose weight
- ❋ Take piano lessons
- ❋ Study impressionist art
- ❋ Take cooking classes in Tuscany
- ❋ Start an herb garden in an indoor window box in the kitchen
- ❋ Improve the lighting in the front hall
- ❋ Adopt a pet
- ❋ Study the complete works of Aristotle
- ❋ Join a gym
- ❋ Take the family on a trip to Greece
- ❋ Study French
- ❋ Be in the presence of His Holiness the Dalai Lama
- ❋ Begin an art collection
- ❋ Take up painting
- ❋ Tutor others in literacy

DO NOT SEEK TO HAVE THAT WHICH HAPPENS HAPPEN AS *YOU* WISH.
WISH THAT WHAT HAPPENS MAY HAPPEN AS IT HAPPENS,
AND YOU WILL BE HAPPY.

Epictetus

Living Takes Time

❋

WE HAVE WHAT WE SEEK. IT IS THERE ALL THE TIME,
AND IF WE GIVE IT TIME, IT WILL MAKE ITSELF KNOWN TO US.

Thomas Merton

Life is a creative, dynamic process. The journey, not the destination, is what we are here to fully appreciate and enjoy. You will never arrive at a place in your life where you're completely satisfied. Your contentment and happiness come from making the most of each experience as you move forward with new goals, desires, and new wishes to fulfill.

Life is all about unfinished business. And living takes time.

Everything takes more time than you think it will. A large percentage of life is taken up with maintenance. We take time to care for ourselves, our spouse, and our children, understanding that neglect of any part of our physical, psychological, or spiritual life will undermine our best intentions. We take care to nourish our relationships with our spouse, family, friends, coworkers, and community. We keep our house, our car, and our appliances in good condition; we have our dishwasher repaired, our lawn fertilized, and our clothes cleaned. In order to support a complex life, we need to devote a great deal of energy to maintenance.

Yet compared to yesteryear, we are blessed with so many time-savers. Think of what it took centuries ago to be able to rise above the arduous necessities of daily living and write an essay or a poem, paint something beautiful or compose harmonious music.

Amidst all of our activities, it's essential to remember that all we have is each day. There are no days that are more important than the one we are now experiencing. Try not to call the things you need to do "chores." Routine domestic tasks are opportunities to make the rhythms of our intimate lives sacred. When we gather at dinner, we break bread together as a sacred act of community. We can pause as we enjoy our food, appreciating all the people who were involved to make our meal possible. Setting up a tea tray in the afternoon creates a meaningful ritual. When we light a fire or a candle, we are opening ourselves to the symbolism of fire as a source of life and creating an atmosphere that is blessed with good energy. Seen in this larger light, everything we do can awaken our souls to appreciation and loving kindness. Approach the ordinary with a sense of abundance, seeing the seeds of transformation in the small humble things we do with a loving attitude.

We may never be able to complete that "to do" list. Don't be consumed by the thousand or so details. Put yourself fully in each thing you choose to do. Be at peace with yourself when you leave errands for another day in order to read a good book or go for a walk in the woods with your dog. Take time to bake chocolate chip cookies, to have a glorious luncheon on a sunny dock, or to have tea with an elderly friend who lives alone.

Learn to make time to take time. Literally, schedule specific times to do the things that add meaning and pleasure to your life. Years ago I called an editor and asked if I could hand deliver a completed manuscript to her. "Can you be here by five-thirty sharp? I'm off to my jazz dance class and I can't be late." I raced against traffic to get there in time to personally hand her my newest book. Off Sally went to her class, carrying my manuscript in my geranium red shopping bag with my logo of a swan spreading its wings and my name printed on the side. By being proactive and deciding ahead of time what you choose to do, and by understanding that living takes time, you'll regularly take time to live.

How do you slow down within a stressful situation when everyone is pressing you to respond, to deliver, and to decide? If you race around, acting frustrated and frantic, chances are you will make mistakes, your judgment will be clouded, and you will take longer to accomplish what needs to be done. Identify what you can do to help, offer suggestions, and remain mindful of whatever you are experiencing in your mind and body. Your turmoil won't help to get things done, so calm yourself.

We can never get it all done, nor should we attempt to do it all. I have learned to leave things undone in order to do other things. I've come back from trips and been so busy upon my homecoming that I literally can't unpack for several days. When this happens, I simply make the apartment off limits to others until I'm able to get caught up. The important thing is to take time to do what you believe are your top priorities. List them in order; you are in charge of your choices.

I've also learned to delegate more to others as I take on exciting projects that keep me on the go. Not only can we learn to leave some things undone, but we can ask others to do some things for us so that we can focus our energies and abilities on the things only we are able to do, the things we do best.

Let someone cook supper for you. Give your children age-appropriate jobs that instill responsibility and save you time. Ask your spouse to run an errand on the way home from work. Peter handles all the faxes to free me to work on other projects. He also handles our travel arrangements, which can be extremely complex.

If something is important to you, make it happen. Otherwise savor the detours; smile if you choose to leave something undone because you prefer something else. Living takes time. Use all there is. Linger in the shower. Stare at the ocean waves. On your evening walk, look up at the stars. Take time to feel humble at the miracle of being here.

I love the well-known saying that happiness is not getting what you want but wanting what you have. Take whatever resources you have to live the life you are destined to live. Take time to be fully present when you are present to take time.

THERE ARE PEOPLE WHO DO NOT LIVE THEIR PRESENT LIFE;
IT IS AS IF THEY WERE PREPARING THEMSELVES, WITH ALL THEIR ZEAL,
TO LIVE SOME OTHER LIFE, BUT NOT THIS ONE. AND WHILE THEY DO
THIS, TIME GOES BY AND IS LOST. WE CANNOT PUT LIFE BACK IN PLAY,
AS IF WE WERE CASTING ANOTHER ROLL OF THE DICE.

Antiphon

Be Careful
What You Give Up

❋

WE CAN DO WHATEVER WE WISH TO DO PROVIDED OUR WISH IS
STRONG ENOUGH. . . . WHAT DO YOU MOST WANT TO DO? THAT'S WHAT
I HAVE TO KEEP ASKING MYSELF IN THE FACE OF DIFFICULTIES.

Katherine Mansfield

Don't give up things you fear you may later regret abandoning. Consider your life now. What would you keep? What will you continue to love or need in your life today? Chapters begin and end in our lives. We are always in stages—uncertain of when the next endings and beginnings will come. Often we don't realize how wonderful something is that soon will be lost. What you have now might be such a precious gift; enjoy everything about it because it is not always going to be there for you.

Visualize what you really want. You need to follow your dreams. Dream more. Keep focused on what you seek from life. Ask yourself, "What am I searching for?" To experience your full potential to your heart's content, think carefully about what you give up. Relinquish only those people, habits, or things that stand in the way of your truest desires and most noble purpose.

What particular things should you decide to keep or to give up?

❋ Your spiritual practice?
❋ Your continuing education?
❋ A job you love but that has obstacles?
❋ Your freedom to express yourself on some sensitive
  political and religious issues?
❋ Some activity you've taken up that has come to affect
  your self-respect?
❋ A small cabin retreat on a lake that you love that
  has become more expensive?
❋ A trusted friend who has just engaged in an indiscretion?
❋ Sitting down to a pretty table for family meals?
❋ Seldom seeing your grandchildren because they live
  far away from you?
❋ Gardening because you think you are too busy to do it?
❋ Baking because you feel there are more important
  things you "should" be doing with your time?
❋ Giving up polishing the brass and silver because it seems
  to be too much work?
❋ Longtime friends because you're engaged in extracurricular
  activities that take up your time and energy?

The best way to live life is to have as few regrets as possible. What you
give up could help or hurt. Be careful what you give up.

YOU'VE GOT ONE LIFE TO LIVE. IT'S SHORT, AT BEST. IT'S A WONDERFUL
PRIVILEGE AND A TERRIFIC OPPORTUNITY—AND YOU'VE BEEN EQUIPPED
FOR IT. USE YOUR *EQUIPMENT*. GIVE IT ALL YOU'VE GOT.

Norman Vincent Peale

Hurry Never

✳

NO MAN WHO IS IN A HURRY IS QUITE CIVILIZED.

Will Durant

We pay a high price when we hurry. We lose our poise and dignity. When we rush, we bang around, grab things, break things, and forget things. Hurrying disconnects us from the gifts that are right in front of us. When we're not mindful, we lose our awareness of what we are doing and what is happening. Have you noticed that people who rush around look angry? They seem to be mad at the world. They're abrupt, even rude. When you're hurrying, you're nervous. You're not having fun. You're not happy, and you're certainly not practicing loving kindness toward others.

The hurried person is exhausting to be around. My mother had a tendency toward anxious rushing that made me feel nervous. It was essentially unloving. The signal was that she was busy and didn't want to be bothered with me; she had "important" things to do. Children don't know how to rush, nor do they understand why anyone does.

People feel slighted by those who rush. The message is that we aren't good enough or important enough to spend time with; their next appointment, person, or event is more significant than we are. These time-urgent people live their lives in an emergency mode. They need to do everything as quickly as possible, as though life were one endless "to do" list.

Rushing is a sign of insecurity. The people I admire the most, those who are my mentors, make me feel as though I'm the most important person in the world; they seem to have all the time in the world to be with me. As a result, I feel uplifted, more confident, more loved.

Whenever we hurry, we disconnect ourselves from ourselves and others. Rushing to the next event kills the gift we now possess. We're less mentally alert because the physical stress of rushing is enervating. Speeding through a stop sign can save a second or two, but if there is an accident, the costs on every level are enormous. Rushing is shortsighted: not only do we make less progress, we lose our perspective.

There are a lot of misguided people who equate time with money. Hurrying, they think, increases their wealth. The truth is they make costly mistakes; they lose their judgment, and they ultimately embrace skewed values. Rushing robs us of the thing we most value: the joyful flow of appreciation of each moment. The precious things money and time can't bring back are forever gone.

It is of considerable consequence that you resist others' pressure to hurry you. It makes me sad to see a child being tugged by a hurried parent. As adults we are responsible for our choices to stay on our path, enjoying every minute of the process. Our final destination is a certainty, and I'm not in a rush to hurry life's journey along. No one can rush you without your consent.

Don't get swept up in others' panic. Remain calm and clearheaded. Take notes if it's appropriate. If you are being pushed to agree to an unrealistic deadline, explain the process of what you need to accomplish and actually add some time to your schedule projections so others won't have unrealistic expectations. I live in the heart of New York City, one of the busiest cities in the world, and I don't get sucked into hurrying because I try to pace myself and plan ahead. Even when I shop or move about, I enjoy walking at my own stride, appreciating the city I love and live in.

How can you handle hurrying when it is unavoidable? I believe hurrying is more avoidable than one might think. We can plan better, be more organized, and calmly think things through. We can avoid hurrying when we don't procrastinate. By setting ourselves up for success, breaking tasks into small steps, we can often avoid last-minute frenzy.

Everything that is great in life is the result of slow, steady growth. Fads last weeks; a philosophy can live for generations. Make slow steady progress. When you don't rush the process, you have time and space for thoughtful reflection and insights. The Chinese sage Lao Tsu reminds us, "The way to do is to be."

What you think and do now builds. Value this moment. Be patient. Smile often. Love the process of living each minute fully. Your presence is a source of strength and an inspiration to people you spend time with. Give your greatest gift—your full attention, yourself.

SUDDENLY I AM AWARE OF EVERY STEP I MAKE.

Thich Nhat Hanh

You Are Smarter and Wiser Than You Think

❋

IT IS CHARACTERISTIC OF WISDOM NOT TO DO DESPERATE THINGS.

Henry David Thoreau

Always remember your brilliance. It is exhilarating to think of your creative contributions, your talents that flow freely through you. Pay attention to your impulses. These sudden inclinations lead us to new insights, new achievements, new learning.

Continue to grow steadily throughout the course of your life. Everything you have thought and done has led you to where you are now, and this richness will continue to build and accumulate. Live each chapter of your life fully and look for the open door to new study, research, and achievement. What you do today might not seem of great significance in the big picture, but it is significant because it is a microcosm of your whole life, your whole experience. Continue to use your fine-tuned mind to produce the thoughts and actions that make you feel good, that bring into your life all that you desire. Trust yourself in all areas of your life.

We tend to judge ourselves rather than promote ourselves. Instead of being purely self-critical, we can try to improve our mind, spirit, and skills while trusting that we do indeed measure up. Human beings have a built-in resilience that can be called on in times of crisis. Through the habit of making wise choices when faced with obstacles, we build our strength of character.

If you encounter a serious problem at work, use it as a way to hone and demonstrate your intelligence and resourcefulness. If you find the circumstances are not appropriate for you to stay, you're free to leave, start your own business, and thrive. A man employed in the corporate world saw dishonesty in the way his company was operating, so he decided to quit and become an art dealer. If a problem arises with an angry family member, one that you feel at a loss to deal with, trust your inner guidance. Exercise forgiveness. Let it go. You can't afford to let any situation destroy your inner peace and happiness because that doesn't help to resolve the problem.

The smartest and wisest way to go through this brief lifetime is to be open and loving, trying to work things out without losing your inner peace, compassion, and understanding. True happiness is the ultimate goal and achievement. What we want is to be in a position to be able to share our happiness, to spread it in a troubled world. By accepting our human nature as well as our divine nature, we can achieve this noble calling.

AWE ENABLES US TO PERCEIVE IN THE WORLD INTIMATIONS OF THE DIVINE, TO SENSE IN SMALL THINGS THE BEGINNING OF INFINITE SIGNIFICANCE, TO SENSE THE ULTIMATE IN THE COMMON AND THE SIMPLE; TO FEEL IN THE RUSH OF THE PASSING THE STILLNESS OF THE ETERNAL.

Rabbi Abraham Joshua Heschel

When You've Made Your Point, Sit Down

※

THERE'S ONE BLESSING ONLY,
THE SOURCE AND CORNERSTONE OF BEATITUDE:
CONFIDENCE IN SELF.

Seneca

This is Peter's mantra—one he seldom follows! When you tell people something and they agree with you, don't keep repeating yourself. Have confidence that when you say something concisely, people will get the message.

Speak directly; eye contact is powerful. Make your point. Sit down.

BREVITY IS THE SOUL OF WIT.

Shakespeare

LET
ALEXANDRA STODDARD
INSPIRE YOUR LIFE

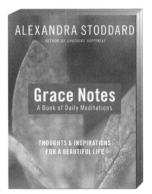
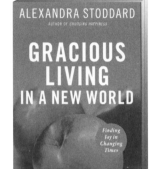
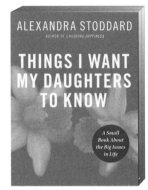

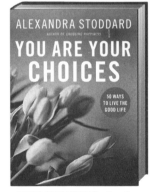